UNINHIBITED, ROBUST, AND WIDE-OPEN

INALIENABLE  RIGHTS SERIES

SERIES EDITOR
Geoffrey R. Stone

GEOFFREY STONE AND OXFORD UNIVERSITY PRESS GRATEFULLY ACKNOWLEDGE THE INTEREST AND
SUPPORT OF THE FOLLOWING ORGANIZATIONS IN THE INALIENABLE RIGHTS SERIES: THE ALA; THE
CHICAGO HUMANITIES FESTIVAL; THE AMERICAN BAR ASSOCIATION; THE NATIONAL CONSTITUTION
CENTER; THE NATIONAL ARCHIVES.

Uninhibited, Robust, and Wide-Open

A FREE PRESS FOR

A NEW CENTURY

Lee C. Bollinger

OXFORD
UNIVERSITY PRESS
2010

OXFORD
UNIVERSITY PRESS

Oxford University Press, Inc., publishes works that further
Oxford University's objective of excellence
in research, scholarship, and education.

Oxford   New York
Auckland   Cape Town   Dar es Salaam   Hong Kong   Karachi
Kuala Lumpur   Madrid   Melbourne   Mexico City   Nairobi
New Delhi   Shanghai   Taipei   Toronto

With offices in
Argentina   Austria   Brazil   Chile   Czech Republic   France   Greece
Guatemala   Hungary   Italy   Japan   Poland   Portugal   Singapore
South Korea   Switzerland   Thailand   Turkey   Ukraine   Vietnam

Published by Oxford University Press, Inc.
198 Madison Avenue, New York, New York 10016

www.oup.com

Oxford is a registered trademark of Oxford University Press

Library of Congress Cataloging-in-Publication Data
Bollinger, Lee C., 1946–
Uninhibited, robust, and wide-open : a free press
for a new century / Lee C. Bollinger.
p.   cm.—(Inalienable rights series)
Includes bibliographical references and index.
ISBN 978-0-19-530439-8
1. Freedom of the press—United States.   I. Title.
KF4774.B66   2010
342.7308'53—dc22   2009023784

1 3 5 7 9 8 6 4 2

Printed in the United States of America
on acid-free paper

For Jean, Lee & Jen, and Carey

Contents

CONTENTS

Acknowledgments

I HAVE MANY people to thank for help and assistance on this book, and it is a great pleasure to be able to single out many of them here. The invitation from Oxford University Press to write a volume on freedom of the press, which I accepted well in advance of a deadline for submission of a manuscript, gave me the opportunity and the challenge over time to think anew about ideas and issues that have occupied my attention for much of my life (beginning as a young boy doing menial tasks in the small-town daily newspaper run by my father). Writing is never a continuous process from start to finish, but there must be some sustained period in which that is your only focus. The trustees of Columbia University made it possible for me to use the summer of 2008 for this purpose. That yielded a draft which I could then periodically return to and build on, as further research and reflection permitted. The editor of the Oxford series on rights, Geoffrey Stone, has been not only a friend and colleague since we met in 1972 but also an outstanding critic and commentator on the First Amendment. Along with his expert comments, I benefited from the thoughtful advice of Oxford Senior Editor David McBride and the careful production by Senior

Production Editor Jessica Ryan. Overseeing and managing the entire process was my outstanding assistant Carla Matero. In Esha Bhandari, Devi Rao, and Jennifer Sokoler, I had the best research assistants one could hope for. And Judith Shulevitz added a perceptive and critical outside editor's eye to help bring the final drafts to completion. Susan Glancy, my Chief of Staff, helped balance the work of the president's office so that writing could find its place.

There were many who generously volunteered to help—giving advice, sharing their expertise, reading and commenting on drafts, listening attentively even to inchoate ideas, giving interviews, and generally sharing their enthusiasm for the project. I am indebted and thankful to every one of these individuals: Floyd Abrams, Steve Adler, Jose Alvarez, Kofi Annan, Vincent Blasi, Alan Brinkley, Robert Burt, Kathleen Carroll, Nigel Chapmen, Kevin Close, David Drummond, Sig Gissler, Don Graham, Kent Greenawalt, Miklos Haraszti, David Ignatius, Merit Janow, Nicholas Lemann, Menachern Mautner, Navanethem (Navi) Pillay, Jeff Sachs, Karl Sauvant, Joseph Sax, Joel Simon, Paul Steiger, David Stone, Gwyneth Williams, and Mark Wood.

Lastly, I wish to thank my wife, Jean. As always, she was there from the beginning to the end—living together the experiences that generated the ideas, happily engaging in conversation about them, and reading and commenting perceptively on the evolving book. Most of all I am forever grateful for the inspiration she continually provides to do right by the world.

I should only note by way of disclosure that I currently serve as a director of The Washington Post Co. It nearly goes without saying that I alone am responsible for everything in this book.

UNINHIBITED, ROBUST, AND WIDE-OPEN

CHAPTER ONE

Uninhibited, Robust, and Wide-Open

THE AMERICAN PRESS, sheltered from censorship by an elaborate body of case law under the First Amendment and sometimes prodded by public regulations to serve the public interest, is one of the greatest achievements of the United States. Wherever you go in the world, journalists envy it. Every year in April, as president of Columbia University, I sit for two days with distinguished journalists to decide which newspapers and reporters will win the Pulitzer prizes in journalism. If you could be there and witness the deliberations (and the painstaking labors of the juries that sift through the nominees and recommend the finalists for each category), you would be struck by the professional standards manifest in the entries and used to select the winners. You would be impressed by the sense of mission that infuses journalists, moved by the dangers they overcome to get their stories, and thankful for the good they accomplish.

Part of what is amazing about journalism in America is that, despite the fact that it operated for most of the twentieth century as a business, it differed from the typical business model in important ways. First, journalism was suffused with a strong sense of mission to serve the public interest. Second, the press was largely able to maintain editorial independence, despite pressures from the state or the commercial interests of their own publications. Third, it was shielded by a constitutional cocoon of protection from the legal accountability ordinarily applicable to comparable businesses. And fourth, much of the media enjoyed the advantages of strong—even monopolistic—economic positions in their markets.

Since the advent of the Internet in the late twentieth century, many American press organizations—particularly newspapers and magazines—have been struggling to remain profitable, and many of them have closed. How American journalism can sustain its autonomy, sense of mission, and a workable financial model has become one of the urgent questions of our time. Nonetheless, America still leads the world in defining journalistic values. For some, it is the model or beacon. For others, it seems appealing but counterintuitive and improbable that a society could organize itself in this way with such a high potential for irresponsibility, instability, and chaos. Still other nations simply envision the role of the press very differently, largely as an arm of the state. And, it must be said, even those that are nearest to the United States in their commitment to a democratic form of government (such as Great Britain, Germany, and France) have sometimes arrived at a different balance when it comes to the press and other societal interests. Unquestionably, the U.S. system evinces an unusual amount of faith in the press and in the public's capacity to shape and use well what the press provides.

It has not always been so. For centuries, English law, from which American law descends, tried to ensure the stability of the state by censoring anything that might undermine the legitimacy of sovereign authority. As speech became more potent, especially through technological advances, so did the laws needed to control it.

A statute from 1352 made it a crime to imagine the king's death, to take up arms against the king, or to "adhere" to the king's enemies. In the seventeenth century, John Twyn, a printer, was convicted of "constructive treason," then hanged, drawn, and quartered for possessing a book arguing that the king was accountable to ordinary citizens, who retained the right to self-government. A statute from 1275 prohibited "any false news or tales whereby discord or occasion of discord or slander may grow between the king and his people."[1] The infamous Star Chamber enforced the law. Sir Edward Coke, in describing a Star Chamber case, famously wrote in 1601 of the law's "three central propositions." These were, first, that a person may be criminally punished for a libel because libel may lead to a breach of the peace; second, that a libel against a government official is a worse offense than a libel of a private individual because it leads to "the scandal of government"; and third, that even though the 1275 statute criminalized the "falsity of the libel," even a true libel may be criminally punished.[2] As one English chief justice said in 1704, "If people should not be called to account for possessing the people with an ill opinion of the government, no government can subsist. For it is very necessary for all governments that the people should have a good opinion of it [*sic*]."[3] By this logic, true statements are potentially more damaging to the public good than false ones (reflected in the maxim that "the greater the truth, the greater the libel"), and, therefore, even true criticisms of public officials could be subject to punishment. Moreover, beginning in 1476 (and lasting until 1694), the English Crown responded to the invention of printing presses by instituting a system of licensing, or "prior restraint," for all publications. In effect, nothing could be published without the prior review and approval of a government censor. This was the American inheritance.

The system in the United States today is very different from this and very much the product of the judicial decisions in the twentieth century and of the social conditions that prevailed then. From the adoption of the First Amendment at the end of the eighteenth century until the beginning of the twentieth century, the press operated without the benefit of major First Amendment protections. Supreme Court decisions regarding freedom of speech and the press began to be handed down early in the twentieth century—in 1919—but these rights only flourished in the second half. Radio and then television (and later cable) emerged midcentury and became key sources of news and information for citizens. The great national experiment of "public interest" regulation of broadcasting developed at the same time. Meanwhile, daily newspapers began to be concentrated in the hands of fewer owners, and most cities found themselves possessed of only one daily newspaper. The notion that the press should serve as the guardian of American democracy, by objectively reporting the news, became an accepted norm. All of these parts interacted to produce a press unique in the world.

Yet, by the close of the twentieth century and the beginning of the twenty-first, major changes were already under way, and the effects of those changes are now in evidence. The history of the world can be seen as the history of the consequences of new forms of human communication and interaction. From the Silk Road to the Gutenberg press to the first transatlantic cable to broadcasting—and now to the Internet—these innovations have launched humanity on courses that no one could have predicted. The impact of the press that we have inherited from the twentieth century remains momentous. But other forces are altering how it functions and the role that it plays in society. The world is rapidly becoming smaller, more intimate, and more interconnected, and the press is both helping to effect this transformation and serving as a primary source of understanding of how we need to shape and manage it.

Today, new communications technologies, principally the Internet and satellites, are vastly expanding the reach of the media, even as globalization is tightening connections among open markets and systems of communication and helping us to perceive issues and problems as transcending national borders. These are, to a very large extent, happy and mutually reinforcing developments. But they are accompanied by a profound irony: Globalization intensifies our need for the press to remain free and independent so that it can report accurately on the world, from the world, to the world. But at the same time, the Internet and other global technologies are undermining the business model that has hitherto kept the press operating, causing a contraction of journalistic engagement with the world, in a world not entirely well situated to foster objective reporting of the news. How will we confront this new, more reactive, and more integrated world with a press weakened by a lack of stable funding and forced to navigate through a bewildering landscape in which the laws governing censorship and access to newsworthy information vary from nation to nation? This book addresses that question.

We have powerful tools with which to begin to answer it: the extraordinary jurisprudence of constitutional law, the public policies directed at enhancing the performance of the press, and the professional culture of journalism. We need to look closely at how these things have developed. This I will do in chapters 1 and 2, principally through the lens of the Supreme Court cases addressing freedom of the press under the First Amendment. To understand how we can create a right to a free press in the twenty-first century, we need to understand how that right was shaped in the twentieth.

In looking back over the Supreme Court decisions of the past century, I see the emergence of three distinct choices. For shorthand, I refer to these choices as the three primary pillars of current First Amendment jurisprudence about freedom of the press. We will examine the cases comprising these pillars, as well as the historical circumstances to which they responded and the outcomes they produced. We will listen to the voices speaking through the decisions, attend the disagreements, and note the roads not taken, because those factors will enlarge our sense of what is possible in the future.

Then, in chapters 3 and 4, we will turn to the present and future. We first need to understand the forces now shaping our world, especially as they relate to our commitment to the principle of freedom of the press. From there, we can begin to formulate an approach that can meet these new challenges. This promises to be an extremely exciting, if daunting, time for a free and independent press. In a sense, I will argue, we need to do on a global stage what was done on the U.S. national stage over the twentieth century. The Supreme Court (and courts generally) continue to have a major role to play, through interpreting the First Amendment. But there are many other levers to be pulled and policies to be fashioned if we are to secure a system of free and independent journalism strong enough to keep good information flowing into the global public forum. More than anything, however, we need to develop a new mindset, a shift in perspective, about what we are trying to do with the right of freedom of the press. No longer can we divide the world into what happens with press freedom in our own country and then view what happens in the rest of the world as "human rights." Now we are all—local press everywhere and new global media—part of a world community looking for understanding about how each part relates to the global whole and about what the global whole itself should be. All of the press is "our" press, because what we need to know will come from these sources. And we need to ensure that the U.S. press is out there in the world reporting on what is important—to the broader world as well as, of course, to Americans. All of this stems from our own self-interest and needs as part of a world community.

What the press will become in the twenty-first century, then, is a matter of utmost importance. It will be the result not only of technological changes and shifting economic tides, but also of the many choices we make about constitutional law, about public policy, about international trade and investment treaties, and about the roles of journalism schools and universities. In this book, I will try to lay out the general perspective and will suggest various actions we might take in this ongoing quest to fulfill the right of a free press.

I

The First Amendment provides that "Congress shall make no law...abridging the freedom of speech, or of the press." These simple words, nowhere elaborated in the Constitution, had no jurisprudence or Supreme Court interpretation behind them until the Court first spoke in 1919 in a series of cases arising out of the suppression of dissent during World War I. Over the ensuing decades, the Court led the judiciary and U.S. society through an extensive process of defining, in practical as well as theoretical ways, what free speech and free press mean in the United States. Before summarizing this jurisprudence, a few preliminary observations are in order.

First, the general process of constitutional adjudication, especially with the First Amendment, is far more than just a matter of setting the boundaries within which the state may act. Law is one of the few areas of public life in which decision makers—in this case, judges and justices—are expected to state principles and reasons for their decisions. This responsibility to explain and justify is coupled with the other great distinguishing characteristic of legal thought: the obligation to follow precedent (or, in the rare decisions in which a court chooses not to follow the holdings of prior cases, to account for sending the law in a different direction). When it comes to the fundamental law of the land—the Constitution—all of this takes on a particularly momentous quality. Constitutional decisions are rooted in society's most basic values and, therefore, breathe life into those values. The Court has the opportunity to speak to the society about its underlying norms and aspirations. What the Court says in explaining its judgments often equals, or even transcends, what it actually decides.

All of this has certainly been true of its opinions about speech and press. The ongoing interplay between the Court's utterances and the broader society, including the press and legislatures, has had much to do with shaping the laws that regulate the press today, even if the causal connections cannot easily be identified.

It is common to think of constitutional law as providing the framework within which an institution like the press can operate freely. But the process of constitutional decision making has broader effects than that. Constitutional law is more than a series of decisions. It can affect the behavior of journalists and of law makers. In trying to grasp the overall state of the press in America, we must be sensitive to the Court's power of persuasion. As a practical matter, the press returns to the Court nearly every year for resolution of yet another issue, so it behooves the press to be the kind of press the Court has said it admires. While it may be difficult to trace this kind of influence, its elusiveness should not be taken as proof that it does not exist.

Another issue that should be highlighted at the outset is the relationship between the twin phrases in the First Amendment: prohibiting the abridgment of "freedom of speech" and the "freedom of the press." Up to this stage in the development of the First Amendment, the Court has seemed to find few differences in the practical import of the two phrases. It seems that the press has all the rights afforded citizens under the Free Speech Clause. What is less clear is whether the Free Press Clause gives the press any rights not available to all citizens. There are numerous decisions denying that the press has unique rights. But this has been a matter of active debate.

One of the strongest proponents for the view that the Free Press Clause gives a "preferred" status for the press was Justice Potter Stewart. In 1975, he wrote an important article arguing for this proposition. "[T]he Free Press guarantee," Stewart began, "is...a *structural* provision of the Constitution."[4] This distinguishes it from "other provisions of the Bill of Rights that protect specific liberties or specific rights of individuals." The free press provision "extends protection to an institution"; indeed, the "publishing business is...the only organized private business that is given explicit constitutional protection." By including such a distinctive entity in the First Amendment, the drafters must have intended for it to have distinctive rights, since "[i]f the Free Press guarantee meant no more than freedom of expression, it would be a constitutional redundancy."[5] Following this line of reasoning and taking into account the important role that the press plays in enhancing the U.S. political system, one can infer that the "primary purpose of the constitutional guarantee of a free press was...to create a fourth institution outside the Government as an additional check on the three official branches," among which the founders "deliberately created an internally competitive system." Accordingly, the press—as recognized by the Constitution itself—is a private institution with a public purpose, a systemic function as vital to American democracy as the three official branches of government (executive, legislative, and judicial). The "relevant metaphor...is that of the Fourth Estate."[6]

The most significant response from within the Court to Justice Stewart's position came in an opinion by Chief Justice Warren Burger in *First National Bank of Boston v. Bellotti* (1978).[7] Burger's opinion rejected the notion of "the Press Clause as somehow conferring special and extraordinary privileges or status on the 'institutional press.'" He offered two arguments for this position. Acknowledging that the history of the First Amendment is less than certain, he found in that background no suggestion "that the authors contemplated a 'special' or 'institutional' privilege," and "most pre–First Amendment commentators who employed the term 'freedom of speech'... used it synonymously with freedom of the press."[8] The second argument was more practical in nature: How are we to define the group entitled to this "special status" of the press? To Burger, this seemed like a dangerous undertaking: "[T]he very task of including some entities within the 'institutional press' while excluding others... is reminiscent of the abhorred licensing system," which "the First Amendment was intended to ban." Better, he concluded, to conceive of the First Amendment as something that "belongs to all who exercise its freedoms," not to "any definable category of persons or entities."[9]

Generally speaking, Chief Justice Burger's approach has thus far carried the day. But there are important qualifications. Certain rights have been recognized by the Court with the press in mind. Even if other citizens can claim the same rights as the press (or, to put it the other way, even if the press has no special or unique rights), that does not mean that those rights were not developed by the Court in order to accommodate the interests of the press.

It should also be noted that the Court has long held that freedom of the press does not mean that the press is exempt from general laws. Thus, in *Associated Press v. NLRB* (1937), the Court confronted a ruling of the National Labor Relations Board that the Associated Press (AP) had violated the National Labor Relations Act (NLRA) when it discharged an employee for engaging in union-organizing activities.[10] The AP at the time was a cooperative organization of the press that gathered news and disseminated it to its 1,350 member newspapers.[11] In a narrow decision of 5–4 decision, the majority held that the application of the NLRA to the AP did not abridge the First Amendment:

The business of the Associated Press is not immune from regulation because it is an agency of the press. The publisher of a newspaper has no special immunity from the application of general laws. He has no special privilege to invade the rights and liberties of others. He must answer for libel. He may be punished for contempt of court. He is subject to the anti-trust laws. Like others he must pay equitable and nondiscriminatory taxes on his business. The regulation here in question has no relation whatever to the impartial distribution of news.[12]

On the other hand, the Court has held that legislatures cannot single out the press, or certain segments of the press, in order to impose regulatory burdens. In *Minneapolis Star & Tribune Co. v. Minnesota Commissioner of Revenue* (1983), for example, the Court considered a Minnesota tax on sales and use. Before 1971, the law exempted periodic publications. In that year, however, the state imposed a "use tax" on the cost of paper and ink products consumed in the production of a periodic publication. As a result, ink and paper used in such publications became the only items subject to the use tax that were components of goods to be sold at retail. This had the effect of disadvantaging only the press. Then, in 1974, the legislature exempted the first $100,000 worth of ink and paper consumed by a publication in any calendar year. This had the effect of taxing only periodic publications with large circulations.[13]

The Court held that the tax violated the First Amendment. The majority reasoned that singling out the press for a tax that did not apply to other persons or businesses created a risk that the press could face the reality or the prospect of taxes directed at it by the government in order to punish or intimidate it. As the Court noted, "even without actually imposing an extra burden on the press, the government might be able to achieve censorial effects, for the threat of sanctions may deter the exercise of First Amendment rights almost as potently as the actual application of sanctions."[14] Further-more, the Court observed that distinguishing among members of the press was constitutionally problematic. By "recognizing a power in the State...to tailor the tax so that it singles out only a few members of the press presents such a potential for abuse that...[Minnesota's interest in an 'equitable' tax system cannot] justify the scheme."[15] The Court concluded that to justify such differential treatment of the press, the state must assert "a counter-balancing interest of compelling importance that it cannot achieve without differential taxation."[16] Similarly, in *Arkansas Writers' Project, Inc. v. Ragland* (1987), the Court held unconstitutional a state statute imposing a sales tax on general interest magazines but not on news-papers or special interest magazines, such as religious, professional, trade, and sports journals. Once again, the Court held that selective taxation of the press raised the potential for unacceptable govern-ment abuse and censorship.[17]

The First Pillar: Extraordinary Protection against Censorship

Now we need to delve into the body of cases that collectively have come to define the American approach to freedom of the press (and freedom of speech as well). The most striking aspect of the first pillar of free press jurisprudence is that protection against censor-ship has been taken to an *extraordinary* level—far beyond what any other society at any time in history has ever recognized. This experiment in the extreme protection of free speech and press is relatively new even in U.S. experience. There have been many explanations for this approach, but, fundamentally, it arises out of an overarching judgment about the proper way to structure the national public forum and through that to best control and moderate natural authoritarian human impulses that can undermine and even destroy a working democratic society.

To understand this pillar, it is necessary to understand a few things about First Amendment doctrine. What is most important is this: In interpreting the First Amendment, the Supreme Court has focused first and foremost on the problem of speech advocating illegal action—such as overthrow of the government through violence or other deliberate disobedience of the law. The key cases arose most often during times of national crisis, particularly World Wars I and II and the Cold War. It is in the crucible of fear and national defense that freedom of speech and press are most severely tested, for it is in such circumstances that a premium is put on patriotism and that dissent is perceived as a direct threat to national security.

The Court initially confronted First Amendment cases during the First World War, and its performance was inauspicious. The Court's announcement of the seemingly rigorous speech-protective standard that purported to forbid censorship unless there was a "clear and present danger" was immediately undermined by a series of decisions that upheld the convictions of dissenters who presented nothing approximating a clear and present danger to the nation. But, as the decades rolled by, the dissenting opinions of great justices such as Oliver Wendell Holmes, Jr. and Louis Brandeis, who eventually argued for a much more robust First Amendment, carried the day. In the McCarthy era, however, the nation again slid into intolerance, and the Court again gave its assent. During the Vietnam War, the Court established its current doctrine. In *Brandenburg v. Ohio* (1969), the Court held unconstitutional—in the context of a Ku Klux Klan rally—a conviction for violating an Ohio statute forbidding advocacy of "crime, sabotage, or unlawful methods of terrorism as a means of accomplishing industrial or political reform."[18] The Court held that "the constitutional guarantees of free speech and free press do not permit a State to forbid or proscribe advocacy of the use of force or of law violation except where such advocacy is directed to inciting or producing imminent lawless action and is likely to incite or produce such action."[19] This is now the heart of the first pillar.

There are, of course, exceptions to the strong principle of protection for speech and press. Certain categories of expression, such as fighting words, threats, commercial advertising, and obscenity, have been held to be of only low First Amendment value and are therefore subject to broader government regulation.[20] Another such category, and a matter of particular concern to the press, is libel, and we now turn to that issue.

Libel

One of the most important First Amendment decisions in the twentieth century, and perhaps of all time, was *New York Times v. Sullivan*, decided by the Court in 1964.[21] Focusing in some depth on this case is helpful to understanding the thinking behind the first pillar. Not only did *New York Times v. Sullivan* set the stage for other issues beyond libel, but it also articulated the central rationale for—and the spirit of—the First Amendment.

For centuries, governments have deemed it essential for society to prohibit the publication of falsehoods that injure an individual's reputation. Throughout American history, the law has extended legal remedies to citizens—primarily through the recovery of damages—for harm to their reputations from false and defamatory statements of fact about them. Although these laws have varied from state to state, all balanced the competing interests by favoring the individual's reputation over the freedom to publish false statements. Indeed, in many states, the reputational interest was so highly valued that all a plaintiff had to do to obtain a judgment and damages was to allege that the defendant had published a defamatory falsehood related to some aspect of his or her life, and damages were then presumed to exist (on the theory that actual damage to a reputation is too difficult to measure). The burden then shifted to the defendant to prove the truth of the statement or the absence of any harm to the plaintiff. If the defendant was found liable, the court or jury could award damages not only to compensate the plaintiff for actual and presumed losses, but also to punish the defendant for publishing a false statement of fact.

Alabama followed this approach in 1960, when the *New York Times* published a paid full-page advertisement by civil rights groups. "Heed Their Rising Voices" was the title of the ad, which appealed for contributions and asserted that authorities in Montgomery County and the State of Alabama had mistreated civil rights protesters.[22] Sullivan at the time was an elected commissioner of the City of Montgomery with the responsibility of oversight of the police department. Though not personally named nor identified in the advertisement, he claimed that the ad falsely accused the police of misbehavior and, by implication, him as well.[23] One passage of the original ad read as follows:

> In Montgomery, Alabama, after students sang "My Country, 'Tis of Thee" on the State Capitol steps, their leaders were expelled from school, and truckloads of police armed with shotguns and tear-gas ringed the Alabama State College Campus. When the entire student body protested to state authorities by refusing to re-register, their dining hall was padlocked in an attempt to starve them into submission.[24]

The advertisement was also an appeal for contributions. Only 394 copies of the paper were distributed in Alabama and just 35 in Montgomery County at the time.[25] The Court noted that the advertisement contained minor errors that were not disputed by the *Times* nor by the four individuals who were also sued as signers of the ad:

It is uncontroverted that some of the statements contained in the two paragraphs were not accurate descriptions of events which occurred in Montgomery. Although [black] students staged a demonstration on the State Capitol steps, they sang the National Anthem and not "My Country, 'Tis of Thee." Although nine students were expelled by the State Board of Education, this was not for leading the demonstration at the Capitol, but for demanding service at a lunch counter in the Montgomery County Courthouse on another day. Not the entire student body, but most of it, had protested the expulsion.... The campus dining hall was not padlocked on any occasion.... Although the police were deployed near the campus in large numbers on three occasions, they did not at any time "ring" the campus.[26]

The jury returned with a verdict against the *New York Times* of $500,000.[27]

The Supreme Court reversed, with Justice William Brennan writing the opinion. Justice Brennan's opinion turned a routine case involving centuries-old common law (clearly in place at the time the framers adopted the First Amendment) into a decision that came to define the very nature of American democracy: "[W]e consider this case against the background of a profound national commitment to the principle that debate on public issues should be uninhibited, robust, and wide-open, and that it may well include vehement, caustic, and sometimes unpleasantly sharp attacks on government and public officials."[28]

The Court spoke of the advertisement "as an expression of grievance and protest on one of the major public issues of our time," observed that false statements are "inevitable in free debate" and "must be protected if the freedoms of expression are to have the breathing space that they need to survive," and insisted that public officials had to be "men of fortitude" able to endure verbal attacks on their dignity and reputation. The Court found a deep lesson in "the court of history" in the conflict over the Sedition Act of 1798, which had made criticism of the government and government officials a crime.[29] The Sedition Act provided that it was a crime "if any person shall write, print, utter or publish any false, scandalous and malicious writings or writings against the government of the United States, or either house of the Congress, or the President, with intent to defame or to bring them…into contempt or disrepute; or to excite against them…the hatred of the good people of the United States."[30] In 1801, President Thomas Jefferson pardoned those convicted, and in later years Congress repaid the fines that had been imposed under the act. This controversy, Brennan said, "crystallized a national awareness of the central meaning of the First Amendment"—that criticism of the government and government officials was at the very heart of the speech protected by the First Amendment.[31]

Providing a mere defense of truth, the Court said, was inadequate under the First Amendment, because truth is often difficult to prove and would-be critics will naturally "steer far wider of the unlawful zone."[32] Valuable speech would therefore be chilled.

Despite the urging of Justices Hugo Black, William O. Douglas, and Arthur Goldberg for a rule of "absolute immunity" for the press "for criticism of the way public officials do their public duty,"[33] the majority announced a lesser level of protection: To recover damages for a false and defamatory statement, a public official must prove that the "statement was made with 'actual malice'—that is, with knowledge that it was false or with reckless disregard of whether it was false or not."[34] Applying this standard to the case, the Court held that the fact that the *Times* had published the advertisement without first checking its own files for news stories that would have revealed the errors was at most "negligence" and not "actual malice."[35]

Sullivan left many important questions open for future resolution: Who counts as a "public official"? What is the kind of "official conduct" to which the "actual malice" standard applies? What constitutes "knowledge" or "reckless disregard" of falsehood? Should there be a burden on the plaintiff to offer proof of actual damages, or can damages be presumed? Should punitive damages in such cases be restricted? Should *Sullivan* lead to the application of the actual malice standard to all discussions of public issues? Or should it be extended only to people who enter the public realm? All of these issues and others have over time been addressed by the Court. The last question, regarding how far the *Sullivan* principle would be extended, was answered ten years later, in 1974, in *Gertz v. Robert Welch, Inc.*[36]

Gertz held that comments about public figures should carry the same protection as those about public officials because, like public officials, "those who attain this status have assumed roles of especial prominence in the affairs of society." Media are therefore "entitled to act on the assumption that public officials and public figures have voluntarily exposed themselves to increased risk of injury from defamatory falsehood concerning them."[37] "Private individuals," on the other hand, can recover damages as long as they establish "negligence" on the part of the media.[38]

The *Sullivan* decision seized the imagination of the First Amendment community. Coming at a time when citizen activism was challenging prevailing laws and practices, the Court's decision had great resonance. It expressed enthusiasm for—not just tolerance of—a public debate that was "uninhibited, robust, and wide-open." It celebrated citizen participation in public discourse and made it unnecessary to fear reprisal for mistakes. It admonished public officials to develop the fortitude to live with harsh and even unfair criticism. And its view of the First Amendment as a national commitment to inverting the usual structure of government, in which sovereignty rests in the state and not in the people, had a joyful quality to it. One of the great scholars of the First Amendment, Harry Kalven, celebrated *Sullivan*'s recognition that the "Amendment has a 'central meaning'—a core of protection of speech without which democracy cannot function, without which, in Madison's phrase, 'the censorial power' would be in the Government over the people and not 'in the people over the Government.'"[39]

Invasion of Privacy

While defamation law dates back centuries, the concept of a legal right of action against the press for publication of private and embarrassing true facts about an individual is comparatively recent in origin. It dates to a famous law review article in 1890, co-authored by Louis Brandeis (before, of course, he became a Justice of the Supreme Court), accusing the press of "overstepping in every direction the obvious bounds of propriety and of decency" by publishing, for example, the "details of sexual relations" and "idle gossip" gathered by "intrusion upon the domestic cycle."[40] Along with this decline in the quality of journalism, the article continued, the rise in the "intensity and complexity of life" has made people "more sensitive to publicity" and in need of "some retreat from the world."[41] These circumstances mandated that the law develop some means of protection.

The law did respond over the next several decades, as state courts and legislatures pursued legal variations on a theme of civil damages for publication of private and embarrassing facts, unless the information was deemed "newsworthy." But this is an area of life where law may do less than it sets out to do. Libel laws protect an individual's reputation against false statement of fact, which means a person might have a strong interest in using the law to set the record straight. Invasion of privacy laws, on the other hand, protect an individual's interest in maintaining the secrecy of certain facts, which means a person may hesitate before bringing a lawsuit and compounding the public revelation. Not surprisingly, then, over time the number of privacy cases has been small compared to the number of libel lawsuits.

In 1975, in *Cox Broadcasting v. Cohn*, the Supreme Court took up the First Amendment implications of these laws.[42] A Georgia statute made it a crime to publish the name or identity of a victim of rape. In a news broadcast by a local television station (owned by Cox Broadcasting Corporation),[43] the name of a teenage girl who had been raped and murdered was revealed. The reporter for the station had discovered the identity of the victim by looking at the official indictment of the youths who were being prosecuted for the crime. To the Court this was a significant fact. Rather than confront the "broader question whether truthful publications may ever be subjected to civil or criminal liability," the majority held, it was clear that the First Amendment protected the "accurate publication of the name of a rape victim obtained from public records—more specifically, from judicial records which are maintained in connection with a public prosecution and which themselves are open to public inspection."[44]

In one sense, the *Cox Broadcasting* decision was only an oblique encounter with the tort of invasion of privacy. Yet, viewed in the context of an era of cases developing extremely strong protections for the press, together with the self-evident fact that broadcasting the identity of a victim is significantly more hurtful than mere disclosure in judicial records, *Cox Broadcasting* is best seen as part of a series of decisions reflecting heightened sensitivity to the need for a free and independent press.

Since *Cox Broadcasting*, the Supreme Court has only twice revisited questions relating to privacy and press freedom. In *The Florida Star v. B.J.F* (1989), the Supreme Court held that imposing damages on a newspaper for publishing the name of a rape victim obtained from a publicly released police report violated the First Amendment.[45]

Next, in *Bartnicki v. Vopper* (2001), the Court found a state's punishment of a newspaper unconstitutional, where the newspaper lawfully obtained a tape of a cellular phone conversation of public concern, and published the tape's contents (even though the telephone call had been illegally intercepted and the reporter knew as much).[46]

State Secrets

Another major case in the lineage of *New York Times v. Sullivan* was the *Pentagon Papers Case* (1971),[47] which involved lawsuits brought by the U.S. government against both the *New York Times* and the *Washington Post*. As with *Sullivan*, the Court's resolution of this controversy put the United States in a unique position in the world of press freedom. The *Pentagon Papers* was a forty-seven-volume history of the U.S. involvement in Southeast Asia, commissioned by Secretary of Defense Robert McNamara in 1967. The document was classified top secret.[48] The *New York Times* and the *Washington Post* received the *Papers* from Daniel Ellsberg, a former Pentagon official who illegally gave them to the press. Upon learning of the leak and the intended publication, the U.S. government filed suits in federal district courts seeking injunctions against publication. The government claimed that public disclosure of the *Papers* would threaten national security, cause the deaths of soldiers, prolong the war in Vietnam, and impair U.S. relations with foreign governments.[49] The Supreme Court rejected these claims as insufficient to overcome the First Amendment presumption of the unconstitutionality of prior restraints. Publication ensued. No further criminal or civil actions were filed against the two newspapers. The government did bring criminal charges against Ellsberg, but the case was dismissed after it was revealed that the government had illegally entered the office of Ellsberg's psychiatrist in search of information about him.[50]

Several of the justices—Black and Douglas in particular—held that national security could not be a mask for suppressing the press.

Justice Black wrote that, under the Constitution, "[t]he press was protected so that it could bare the secrets of government and inform the people."[51] Justice Douglas added that "[s]ecrecy in government is fundamentally anti-democratic, perpetuating bureaucratic errors. Open debate and discussion of public issues are vital to our national health."[52] Justice Brennan said that the Court could uphold the injunction only if the government proved that "publication must inevitably, directly, and immediately cause the occurrence of an event kindred to imperiling the safety of a transport already at sea."[53] Sympathy for the government's need for secrecy grew as other justices weighed in. Justices Potter Stewart and Byron White argued that the government could enjoin speech if it could establish that disclosure would "surely result in direct, immediate, and irreparable damage to our Nation or its people."[54]

The *Pentagon Papers* ascended into the pantheon of First Amendment cases protecting freedom of the press. But it, too, left many questions unanswered. When is the publication of classified information sure to lead to "immediate and irreparable" national injury? And, even though the government would be precluded from obtaining an *injunction* against publication (i.e., a prior restraint), could it still successfully bring a criminal prosecution after publication?

We have now lived in a *Pentagon Papers* world for a half century. The government continues to seek and to find ways to keep information secret, partly by overclassifying information. The press continues to search for and to find government employees willing to leak classified information, and then it decides whether to publish. Over time, the government has chosen not to go to court seeking injunctions or criminal or civil penalties against the press for receiving or publishing official secrets. On the other hand, every administration has sought to clamp down on government leakers. Rarely, though, are leakers successfully identified, and even more rarely are they prosecuted. In only one case, in fact, has the government managed to convict a leaker.[55]

Fair Trial

Another landmark decision involved the conflict between the Sixth Amendment right of an individual to a fair and impartial trial when charged with a crime and the First Amendment right of a free press to publish information about a criminal prosecution. In 1976, the Supreme Court confronted this conflict in *Nebraska Press Association v. Stuart*. The defendant in this case had been charged with murdering several people in a rural town.[56] The case was notorious and generated intense media interest. Because of this, the state court judge ordered newspapers and broadcasters not to publish any stories about the confessions of the defendant nor any other facts "strongly implicative" of the defendant.[57] The press challenged this order. The Supreme Court ruled unanimously that the order violated the First Amendment.

The Court conceded that the trial judge was "justified in concluding that there would be intense and pervasive pretrial publicity concerning this case" and that the "publicity might impair the defendant's right to a fair trial."[58] But the Court held that the judge had not sufficiently explored whether other means could have been used to protect the defendant's right to a fair trial. These other means included changing the venue of the trial, postponing it, screening out jurors whose judgment might have been infected by the coverage, giving clear instructions to jurors to ignore the coverage, sequestering the jury, restricting what participants in the trial process (lawyers, police, etc.) could tell the press, and closing the trial itself.[59]

In a separate opinion, Justice Brennan declared that a fundamental tenet of the First Amendment is that "discussion of public affairs in a free society cannot depend on the preliminary grace of judicial censors." Justice Brennan observed: "The press may be arrogant, tyrannical, abusive, and sensationalist, just as it may be incisive, probing, and informative. But...the decision of what, when, and how to publish is for editors, not judges."[60]

So, the first pillar of First Amendment jurisprudence in the twentieth century reflected a clear choice on the part of the Court to extend freedom of the press to its outer limits. Every decision that contributed to this pillar was qualified in ways that would make pulling back in the future possible. But the overall thrust of these holdings, underscored by a passion for a largely unbounded national forum, has created an extraordinary zone of protection for the press.

The Second Pillar: No Right of Access to Information

When it comes to the second pillar of freedom of the press, we find that the Court, in interpreting the First Amendment, has gone in the opposite direction. In case after case, the Court has been unwilling to recognize robust rights of the press in the newsgathering process, especially when the press has sought to gain access to information held or controlled by the government.

The press's argument for special rights in the newsgathering arena is straightforward: Because so much newsworthy information is under the control of the state, the press cannot perform its assigned role unless the courts interpret the First Amendment as encompassing the right to gain access to information commensurate with the right to publish that information. The right to speak means little without access to the relevant information. This seems to be a compelling argument. But, with one exception, the Court has declined to heed it.

In *Pell v. Procunier* (1974), reporters sought to have face-to-face interviews with prison inmates in order to report on their mistreatment. The Court rejected the claim:

> It is one thing to say that...the government cannot restrain the publication of news....It is quite another thing to suggest that the Constitution imposes upon government the affirmative duty to make available to journalists sources of information not available to members of the public generally. That proposition finds no support in the words of the Constitution or in any decision of this Court.[61]

Four justices dissented. Justice Douglas (joined by Justices William Brennan and Thurgood Marshall) argued that, because the "public's interest in being informed about prisons [is] paramount," it is "not enough to note that the press [is] denied no more access to the prisons than is denied the public generally." To the contrary, the "absolute ban on press interviews with [inmates] is far broader than is necessary to protect any legitimate governmental interests and is an unconstitutional infringement on the public's right to know protected by the free press guarantee of the First Amendment."[62]

Decisions like *Pell v. Procunier* stopped the press's claim for special access in its tracks.[63] But the most famous case on the newsgathering front, *Branzburg v. Hayes* (1972), was decided two years before *Pell*. The Court's decision rejected the press's argument that the First Amendment grants reporters a constitutional right not to reveal the identities of their sources in grand jury or other criminal proceedings.[64] To journalists, confidentiality is a cornerstone of effective reporting, since anonymity is to leakers what robust protection against censorship is to speakers. *Branzburg* involved several cases in which reporters had been called before grand juries to testify about their sources for stories they had written on, for example, illegal drug activities. Each of the reporters had refused, and each had been held in contempt of court.[65] The reporters asked not for an absolute privilege but rather for a principle that reporters "should not be forced either to appear or to testify before a grand jury or at trial until and unless sufficient grounds are shown for believing that...the information the reporter has is unavailable from other sources, and that the need for the information is sufficiently compelling to override the claimed invasion of First Amendment interests occasioned by the disclosure."[66]

The Court began by observing: "It has generally been held that the First Amendment does not guarantee the press a constitutional right of special access to information not available to the public generally." The Court noted that "the press is regularly excluded from grand jury proceedings, our own conferences, the meetings of other official bodies gathered in executive session, and the meetings of private organizations." Moreover, reporters "have no constitutional right of access to the scenes of crime or disaster when the general public is excluded."[67]

The Court then held that, in the *Branzburg* case, there was "no basis" for finding that the "public interest in law enforcement...is insufficient to override the...burden on news gathering that is said to result from insisting that reporters...respond to relevant questions."[68] The Court denied that "there would be a significant constriction of the flow of news to the public" in the absence of a constitutional privilege.[69] And it expressed concern about the "practical and conceptual difficulties" in defining "those categories of newsmen who qualified for the privilege, a questionable procedure in light of the traditional doctrine that liberty of the press is the right of the lonely pamphleteer...just as much as of the large metropolitan publisher."[70]

Justice Lewis Powell issued a crucial concurring opinion, which was meant to temper the Court's decision. Powell insisted that if a reporter has "reason to believe that his testimony implicates confidential source relationships without a legitimate need of law enforcement...an appropriate protective order may be entered."[71]

Justice Stewart wrote a dissenting opinion, joined by Justices Brennan and Marshall. In his view, the Court had taken a "crabbed view of the First Amendment" that "reflects a disturbing insensitivity to the critical role of an independent press in our society."[72] For Justice Stewart and his colleagues, "[a] corollary of the right to publish must be the right to gather news.... [The] right to gather news implies, in turn, a right to a confidential relationship between a reporter and his source."[73] Justice Stewart rejected the idea that the press should have to present "empirical" evidence of a disruption in the flow of information because of compelled disclosures. "Common sense," he contended, is sufficient foundation for the Court to protect constitutional rights."[74] Stewart argued that in order for the government to force the release of confidential information, the state should have to demonstrate "a compelling and overriding interest" in the information, that the information could not "be obtained by alternative means," and that there was "probable cause" to believe that the journalist has information that is clearly relevant to a specific probable violation of law.[75]

Branzburg continues to govern the constitutional issue of requiring reporters to disclose information, including the identities of their confidential sources. Subsequent to *Branzburg*, however, most states have enacted shield laws that protect reporters against orders to disclose. These laws vary significantly in the scope of protection they afford reporters.[76] At this moment, the U.S. Congress is considering a federal shield law.[77]

There is one important exception to the Court's negative stance toward a newsgathering right. In *Richmond Newspapers v. Virginia*

(1980), the question was whether the public and the press have the right to attend criminal trials.[78] The lineup of the justices reflected a broad consensus on the fundamental need for a newsgathering right but a lack of consensus on how to develop such a new right. Chief Justice Burger announced the Court's decision and wrote an opinion for himself and Justices Byron White and John Paul Stevens. Justices Brennan and Marshall wrote separately, concurring in the judgment, as did Justice Stewart. Justice William Rehnquist dissented.

Burger stressed the historical practice of conducting open criminal trials and noted several benefits of such a custom, including greater public confidence in the criminal justice system and better decisions in trials.[79] Moreover, he acknowledged that, if there were no protection for news gathering, freedom of the press could be "eviscerated."[80] *Pell* and similar cases were, in his view, distinguishable because they involved prisons which, "by definition, are not 'open' or public places," unlike courts. Burger emphasized, however, that the right being recognized applied equally to the public and the press. That is, closing a criminal trial violates the right of the public to attend, without recognizing any special right of the press.

Justice Brennan (joined by Justice Marshall) argued that the First Amendment "has a *structural* role to play in securing and fostering our republican system of self-government."[81] Not only must debate be robust, but "public debate [must] be informed." So, the First Amendment must concern itself not only with communication, but also with "the indispensable conditions of meaningful communication." But, Brennan admitted, this argument is "theoretically endless."[82] Some limiting principles are needed, or the First Amendment would give the press access to all government information. One possible limiting principle is tradition: If information has been available in the past, it should be now. Tradition, Brennan reasoned, "implies the favorable judgment of experience." Another limiting principle, he suggested, is whether having access to the information sought is "important" to the functioning of government. This was true in *Richmond Newspapers*, he reasoned, because open trials enhance the system of justice.[83]

Richmond Newspapers remains the only exception to the second pillar of First Amendment jurisprudence.[84]

The Third Pillar: Regulating the Press to Improve the Press

We turn now to the third and final course chosen by the Supreme Court in the twentieth century. It is the one most often overlooked when people talk about the tradition of freedom of the press in America.

Broadcasting: Radio and Television

It all started in 1927 with a congressional statute to regulate the new medium of radio. This first step evolved into the Communications Act of 1934, which remains to this day the governing legislation for the regulation of radio and television. The act authorized the government to take and to keep control over channels of "radio transmission; and to provide for the use of such channels, but not the ownership thereof, by persons for limited periods of time."[85] It created the Federal Communications Commission (FCC) and charged it with the authority to implement a licensing and regulatory regime governing use of the broadcast spectrum "as public convenience, interest, or necessity requires."[86] Over succeeding decades, the FCC built up an elaborate system for awarding licenses to individual radio and television stations based on a decision to allocate the electromagnetic spectrum in ways that favored local rather than national stations. Keeping in mind the "public interest" standard, the FCC created regulations designed to expand the amount of information and the range of viewpoints that would reach the public. The most significant of those regulations was the Fairness Doctrine, which required each broadcaster to provide coverage of "controversial issues of public importance"[87] and to present "opposing viewpoints as a condition of retaining its license."[88] Corollary doctrines mandated that broadcasters give citizens the opportunity to respond if they were attacked or criticized in the course of broadcast editorials (the "personal attack" rule) and grant airtime to candidates for public office whose opponents had been endorsed by licensees (the "political editorial" rule).[89]

The Fairness Doctrine was the creation of the FCC, but the 1934 act explicitly included other similar rules. The "equal time" provision provided that candidates for public office must be offered equal time whenever licensees gave their opponents an opportunity to speak. And the "reasonable access" rule required licensees to give candidates for federal office a reasonable opportunity to purchase airtime.[90]

The Fairness Doctrine had the potential to become a powerful lever in political debates, and in the 1960s and '70s, it became one. Activist groups of all kinds—especially those with fewer resources— invoked the Fairness Doctrine to counter ideas they opposed. Environmental groups wanted airtime to answer advertisements for automobiles. Anti-smoking advocates demanded the right to respond to cigarette advertisements. Anti-war groups tried to rebut advertisements for military recruiting. Civil rights activists advanced the doctrine to advocate racial justice. Consumer advocates did so in their effort to enact bottle-return laws.

Perhaps surprisingly, the constitutionality of the Fairness Doctrine was not challenged until 1969, in the landmark case of *Red Lion Broadcasting Co. v. FCC*. The facts of *Red Lion* were revealing about the power and scope of the public regulatory regime for broadcasting. A minor radio station in Pennsylvania had broadcast a program by a conservative commentator, the Reverend Billy James Hargis, in which Hargis strongly criticized liberal author Fred J. Cook for his book *Goldwater: Extremist on the Right*. Hargis leveled various charges against Cook, including that, while working at a newspaper, he had falsely charged city officials, for which he had been fired; that he had associated with communists; and that he intended to "smear and destroy" Goldwater.[91] Some years after *Red Lion*, former CBS News president Fred Friendly (by then a professor at the Columbia School of Journalism) wrote of how Cook's Goldwater book had been funded by the Democratic National Committee (DNC). The DNC also regularly monitored right-wing broadcasts and filed complaints under the Fairness Doctrine whenever it could—which it did in the case of the Hargis broadcast, demanding free time to reply under the personal-attack rule.[92]

In a unanimous decision, the Court in *Red Lion* issued a resounding affirmation of the Fairness Doctrine (which by 1969 had also been applied to the new technology of television). The Court began with a summation of the broadcaster's argument: Under the First Amendment, broadcasters have the same rights as anyone to say "whatever they choose, and to exclude whomever they choose from ever using that frequency." Just as "[n]o man may be prevented from saying or publishing what he thinks, or from refusing in his speech or other utterances to give equal weight to the views of his opponents," the same "right, they say, applies equally to broadcasters."[93]

The Court began by explaining the basis on which the issue had to be approached: "Although broadcasting is clearly a medium affected by a First Amendment interest, differences in the characteristics of new media justify differences in the First Amendment standards applied to them."[94] Then the Court proceeded to identify the differences it perceived between broadcasting and print media. It observed that the electromagnetic spectrum—through which all broadcast signals must pass—could accommodate only a limited number of users. This required an allocation scheme:

> Where there are substantially more individuals who want to broadcast than there are frequencies to allocate, it is idle to posit

an unabridgeable First Amendment right to broadcast comparable to the right of every individual to speak, write, or publish.... It would be strange if the First Amendment, aimed at protecting and furthering communications, prevented the Government from making radio communication possible by requiring licenses to broadcast and by limiting the number of licenses so as not to overcrowd the spectrum.[95]

In other words, the government had to intervene in order to avoid what otherwise would be chaos from conflicting broadcast signals.

The Court considered it reasonable for those fortunate few who had been awarded a license to be subject to public oversight in order to keep them from abusing this privilege. Although the government could not censor broadcasts, it could act to ensure that the public received the full range of information and ideas:

A license permits broadcasting, but the licensee has no constitutional right to...monopolize a radio frequency to the exclusion of his fellow citizens. There is nothing in the First Amendment which prevents the Government from requiring a licensee to share his frequency with others and to conduct himself as a proxy or fiduciary with obligations to present those views and voices which are representative of his community and which would otherwise, by necessity, be barred from the airwaves.[96]

The Court added that it is "the right of the viewers and listeners, not the right of the broadcasters, which is paramount." Indeed, what is "crucial" in this environment "is the right of the public to receive suitable access to social, political, [a]esthetic, moral, and other ideas and experiences."[97] To hold otherwise, the Court concluded, would mean that "station owners and a few networks would have unfettered power to make time available only to the highest bidders" and to transmit only the views they preferred. This would be "unlimited private censorship."[98]

Red Lion was a striking and forceful affirmation of the role of public regulation in preserving the vitality of the marketplace of ideas. As such, it highlighted the next major question: Would this apply to daily newspapers, as well? The Court gave its unanimous—and negative—answer to that question five years later in *Miami Herald v. Tornillo* (1974).

Florida had enacted a "right of reply" statute providing that, if "a candidate for [political office] is assailed regarding his personal character or official record by any newspaper, the candidate has the right to demand that the newspaper print, free of cost to the candidate, any reply the candidate may make to the newspaper's charges." The statute specified that the reply had to "appear in as conspicuous a place and in the same kind of type as the charges which prompted the reply, provided it does not take up more space than the charges."[99] Although this statute was in the same vein as the "political editorial" corollary of the Fairness Doctrine, the Court rejected the Florida law out of hand without ever mentioning *Red Lion*.

The Court started by recounting the state's argument that newspapers had "become big business," "noncompetitive," and "enormously powerful" in their ability to "manipulate public opinion." Contributing to this state of affairs, Florida argued, were the economic realities of the newspaper business. Large economies of scale had made it nearly impossible for new newspapers or magazines to launch.[100] As a result, the number of newspapers had declined precipitously, and most towns and cities now had only one newspaper, which had extraordinary influence on public opinion. The statute was designed to rectify that state of affairs.

The Court held that the First Amendment was an absolute barrier to such regulation: "However much validity may be found in these arguments...the implementation of a remedy such as an enforceable right of access" is incompatible with the First Amendment.[101] The government, the Court reasoned, may not compel editors or publishers to publish material "that 'reason tells them should not be published.'"[102] Not only might journalists censor themselves in order to avoid having to publish replies, but even if they did not, the Florida statute was unacceptable because it intruded on the decision-making process of editors.[103]

To this day, *Red Lion* and *Miami Herald* remain the constitutional linchpins for thinking about regulations of the media to promote what is thought to be the public interest. In 1987, however, the FCC formally repealed the Fairness Doctrine, asserting that the regulation was inconsistent with the First Amendment because it chilled broadcaster expression.[104] The commission said that it favored the market as a means of allocating opportunities for speech. The chair of the FCC at the time, Mark Fowler, reflecting the anti–government regulation philosophy of the Ronald Reagan administration, described television as "just another appliance." It was, he added, "a toaster with pictures."[105] All other regulations (e.g., the equal time provision, and general public interest standards) have remained in place.[106]

There is one more notable broadcasting case involving public access and media, *Columbia Broadcasting System v. Democratic National Committee* (1973). Suits against broadcasters had been brought by two parties—the DNC and the Business Executives Move for Vietnam Peace (BEM)—which claimed that, under the First Amendment and under the "public interest" standard of the 1934 Communications Act, private citizens and groups have a right to purchase airtime in order to address public issues. Broadcasters had (and still have) a policy of declining to sell airtime for controversial public-issue speech, believing that audiences would change channels when confronted with political speech they dislike or that broadcasters would be sued for things such as libel (as the *New York Times* was in *Sullivan*). By a narrow majority, the Court rejected the claims of the DNC and BEM, holding that such groups have no First Amendment right to purchase airtime. In other words, Congress can constitutionally require licensees to present certain speech, but the First Amendment doesn't of its own force compel broadcasters to sell airtime to others.[107]

To complete the review of cases in the third pillar, we need to take a quick look at government-sponsored broadcasting, cable, and the Internet.

Public Broadcasting

One of the great questions under the First Amendment generally, and one that has particular relevance to the principle of freedom of the press, is: What powers over content does the government retain when it funds the press? One might think that, after all, if public funds are provided, then public control ought to follow logically. Americans should want our government, which for good or for bad represents us as a nation, to engage in expression, and it has the same interest as private speakers to avoid the appearance of endorsing views with which it disagrees. At the same time, public funding of expressive activities is so vast and often so needed for a vibrant marketplace of ideas (for the arts, for academic research, etc.) that, unless the First Amendment imposes a barrier against state interference, the corrupting and distorting power of censorship will manifest itself through controls exacted through the use of the public purse. In *FCC v. League of Women Voters* (1984), the Supreme Court notably confronted this question and chose to provide significant protection against government control of the content of public broadcasting.

The modern system of public broadcasting in the United States dates to 1967 with the enactment of the Public Broadcasting Act.

Under section 399 of the act, public broadcasting stations that received grants from the Corporation for Public Broadcasting were forbidden from "engag[ing] in editorializing."[108] The purpose of the provision was both to prevent the government from using its funding power to influence editorial content and to prevent private interest groups from capturing these stations, causing them "to express their own partisan viewpoints."[109] The Court held that because section 399 prohibited broadcasters "from speaking out on public issues," it constituted a "substantial abridgment of important journalistic freedoms which the First Amendment...protects."[110]

Cable

Cable television posed another set of challenges. In its early decades (the 1950s and 1960s), cable brought broadcasting signals both to remote parts of the country otherwise not accessible by existing stations and to large cities where tall buildings sometimes caused interference. The promise of cable technology to expand the range of available channels was much remarked upon by the early 1970s, and the prospect of dozens and even hundreds of channel options seemed an unbelievable bounty of potential programming.

But radio and network television were not particularly welcoming to cable. In the 1960s, the FCC, out of concern for broadcasters, asserted jurisdiction over cable on the theory that cable affected broadcast signals. Just as the print media for decades had never regarded broadcasters as real journalists and never came to their defense when broadcast regulations were challenged as abridgments of freedom of the press, so broadcasters were quick to assert that the FCC must seize jurisdiction over cable in order to "protect" the "public interest."[111] Because cable technology required the laying of cables, either from existing telephone poles or under the ground, including under public streets, local communities argued that they could properly regulate this new industry. Thus, both the FCC and cities throughout the country claimed regulatory authority over cable television.

There was much discussion about how the scarcity rationale of *Red Lion* would evaporate for television once cable created hundreds of channels, but complicating this argument was the fact that cable was, and remains, virtually a monopoly in every city where it exists. Cable is a medium with many channels but only one owner. The de facto monopoly status of cable in every city was the result of a licensing process that limited the franchise to one owner, but most economists reasoned that cable was a "natural monopoly" and that open competition would therefore not have resulted in multiple companies.[112] In this sense, cable was arguably analogous to the situation that had "naturally" developed with newspapers.

In 1994, the Court examined how cable technology fits with the First Amendment. The Cable Television Consumer Protection and Competition Act of 1992 required cable television companies to carry without charge the signals of local broadcast television stations. In *Turner Broadcasting System, Inc. v. FCC* (1994), the Court noted that Congress had found:

> [T]he overwhelming majority of cable operators exercise a monopoly over cable service [and]…this market position gives cable operators the power and the incentive to harm broadcast competitors. The power derives from the cable operator's ability [to refuse to transmit broadcast signals]. The incentive derives from the economic reality that "[c]able television systems and broadcast television stations increasingly compete for television advertising revenues." By refusing carriage of broadcasters' signals, cable operators…can reduce the number of households that have access to the broadcasters' programming, and thereby capture advertising dollars that would otherwise go to broadcast stations.[113]

In such circumstances, "Congress concluded that unless cable operators are required to carry local broadcast stations, '[t]here is a substantial likelihood that...the economic viability of free local broadcast television...will be seriously jeopardized.'"[114]

The justices issued multiple opinions, but there was general agreement that cable television regulation should be subject to a different standard than broadcast regulation under the First Amendment. In Justice Anthony Kennedy's opinion for the Court, he observed that broadcast cases are "inapposite" because cable technology does not suffer the limitations that hobbled broadcast technology: "Indeed, given the rapid advances in fiber optics and digital compression technology, soon there may be no practical limitation on the number of speakers who may use the cable medium. Nor is there any danger of physical interference between two cable speakers attempting to share the same channel." Justice Kennedy argued that the "more relaxed standard of scrutiny" adopted in *Red Lion* should not apply to the regulation of cable.[115]

The government argued that "market dysfunction" in the cable world should be sufficient to justify government regulation. The Court conceded that "the cable market suffers certain structural impediments" but insisted that it was only "the special physical characteristics of broadcast transmission, not the economic characteristics of the broadcast market," that the Court in *Red Lion* had found material in its First Amendment analysis. "The mere assertion of dysfunction or failure in a speech market, without more," the Court reasoned, "is not sufficient to shield a speech regulation from the First Amendment standards applicable to nonbroadcast media."[116] Neither Justice Kennedy's opinion nor any of the others explained why the "market dysfunction" that yields a practical monopoly should be treated differently from the "special physical characteristics of broadcast transmission."

In a dissent, Justice Sandra Day O'Connor wrote an opinion joined by Justices Antonin Scalia, Ruth Bader Ginsburg, and Clarence Thomas, dissenting in part. Justice O'Connor began by acknowledging the broader significance of the majority's holding: "It is as if the government ordered all movie theaters to reserve at least one-third of their screening for films made by American production companies, or required all bookstores to devote one-third of their shelf space to nonprofit publishers." The must-carry rule raised two concerns from a First Amendment perspective, according to Justice O'Connor. It ordered cable operators to carry programming they preferred not to carry and denied cable operators "access to over one-third of an entire medium."[117]

The last case that fleshes out the Court's view of cable within the purview of the First Amendment is *Denver Area Educational Telecommunications Consortium, Inc. v. FCC,* decided in 1996. In *Denver,* the Court reviewed several provisions of the Cable Act of 1992 that dealt with "indecent" programming, defined as programming that depicts or describes "sexual...activities or organs in a patently offensive manner."[118]

Congress has long regulated "indecent" speech in broadcasting. The Supreme Court upheld this regulation in its 1978 decision in *FCC v. Pacifica Foundation. Pacifica* involved an afternoon radio broadcast of George Carlin's famous comedy monologue entitled "Filthy Words" (which repeatedly used "seven dirty words" that cannot be said on television or radio). The FCC fined the station. Citing *Red Lion* and emphasizing that broadcasting enters the home, where "privacy" interests are paramount and children are present, the Court held that, at least in the special circumstances of broadcasting, the government could constitutionally limit "indecent" programming to certain times of the day.[119]

Pacifica stands in sharp contrast to a Supreme Court case from the 1970s about indecent language in public spaces. In *Cohen v. California*

(1971), the Court held unconstitutional a California law used to punish a person for wearing a jacket with the words "Fuck the Draft" written on the back. The Court explained that the use of profanity is useful to express the "emotive" content of speech, that Americans have to be prepared to confront such speech in public places, and that there is no discernible principle by which courts could determine whether speech was too "offensive" to deserve constitutional protection.[120]

In the *Denver* case, the Court distinguished cable from broadcasting and invalidated a section of the 1992 act that required cable operators to put "indecent" programming on a single channel and block it from viewers unless the subscriber gave a written request to unblock it.[121] In 1996, Congress enacted a new law that required cable operators to "fully scramble" or limit transmission to restricted times for any channels "primarily dedicated to sexually-oriented programming." In 2000, the Court invalidated this law.[122]

In the *Denver* case, the Court also reviewed provisions of the Cable Communications Policy Act of 1984 authorizing local governments to require cable operators to set aside channels for "public, educational, or governmental use," while prohibiting any editorial control of these public-access channels. The Court held this provision unconstitutional. The most interesting discussion among the justices concerned general approaches for dealing with new technologies of communication, and cable in particular, under the First Amendment. Justice David Souter spoke of the state of "flux" in cable, which he thought called for a case-by-case, fact-based approach. Justices Kennedy and Ginsburg argued for applying general principles of First Amendment analysis. Justice Thomas, joined by Justices Rehnquist and Scalia, argued that "the operator's right...is preeminent."[123]

One last area of the public regulation of media worth noting consists of rules limiting media ownership in order to maximize the number of available voices. For some decades now, the FCC has had policies about the number of broadcast stations a single entity can own, nationally and in any single market, and about the "cross-ownership" of both newspapers and broadcast stations in a single market. These policies are very complex. In *FCC v. National Citizens Committee for Broadcasting* (1978), the Supreme Court upheld cross-ownership regulations on the grounds that "the Commission has long given 'primary significance' to 'diversification of control of the media of mass communications.' "[124] The policy was deemed to be consistent "with the First Amendment goal of achieving 'the widest possible dissemination of information from diverse and antagonistic sources.' "[125] Opponents of the regulation argued that it restricted both broadcasters' and newspapers' opportunities for expression. Quoting *Red Lion*, the Court answered that "to deny a station license because 'the public interest' requires it 'is not a denial of free speech.' "[126] The Court concluded that the "regulations are a reasonable means of promoting the public interest in diversified mass communications; thus they do not violate the First Amendment rights of those who will be denied broadcast licenses pursuant to them."[127]

The Internet

Finally, there is the Internet and freedom of the press. In *Reno v. American Civil Liberties Union* (1997), the Court held unconstitutional parts of the Communications Decency Act of 1996 that prohibited transmitting over the Internet any "indecent" material or any material that "depicts or describes, in terms patently offensive as measured by contemporary community standards, sexual or excretory activities or organs" in a manner that might reach someone under eighteen years of age.[128] The Court distinguished the Internet from broadcasting:

> [E]ach medium of expression...may present its own problems.
> Thus, some of our cases have recognized special justifications

for regulation of the broadcast media that are not applicable to other speakers [citing *Red Lion* and *Pacifica*]. In these cases, the Court relied on the history of extensive Government regulation of the broadcast medium, the scarcity of available frequencies at its inception, and its "invasive" nature. Those factors are not present in cyberspace.[129]

The Court noted that the Internet "provides relatively unlimited, low-cost capacity for communication of all kinds." Thus, "our cases provide no basis for qualifying the level of First Amendment scrutiny that should be applied to this medium."[130]

II

It is often assumed that constitutional law exists in its own orbit of logic: determined by the history of the clause being applied, shaped by textual interpretation, and governed by precedent. Like cases are treated alike, and principle demands a uniformity of results across similar fact patterns. Deeper values embodied in the constitutional document manifest themselves in particular decisions, and the courts do not try through the cases to inspire and create those values. An opposing view sees none of these constraints and rather surmises that history, text, and precedents are so vague and subject to manipulation that the decisions reached are nothing more than the personal preferences of the justices or mere reflections of the political conditions of the era.

I will not speak about other constitutional provisions, but the case law that comprises the jurisprudence of freedom of speech and press is much more nuanced, ambitious, and strategic than any of the standard theories would suppose. The decisions certainly are not removed from the social contexts in which they occurred; at critical times they even play off of the realities on the ground and embrace and encourage public policies that have emerged from a society struggling toward the same ends as the Court. Nor are they determined by them. They are instead best seen as part of a large and complicated process of creating a particular kind of national public forum, in which the press is conceived as playing a vital role, for the purpose of helping the society to deal with an increasingly diverse and pluralistic political system. Grasping that complex process and agenda is the subject of the next chapter and the basis for projecting the principle of freedom of the press into the twenty-first century.

CHAPTER TWO

It Is an Experiment

DURING THE TWENTIETH CENTURY, both the press and press freedom underwent enormous and unprecedented transformations. In the first decade of the twenty-first century, as communications technology changes radically and the world becomes increasingly integrated, which expands our need for the press and transforms and undermines it at the same time, both the press and its freedoms are undergoing changes of similar magnitude. This seems a good moment to step back and ask: Did the choices and decisions of the twentieth century make sense? Were they reasonable responses to the policies and circumstances of that era, or were they driven by the unreflective impulses of the moment?

In law, as in life, we often respond intuitively to specific problems or cases, and an overarching rationale emerges only later when we pause and reflect on what we have done. The reaction of the moment hides a deeper reasoning, itself revealed only with the passage of time and changes in perspective. This is the essence of the common-law tradition: We build up over time a body of concrete decisions in the context of real disputes—giving the best explanation available for each case and building on earlier decisions (following, distinguishing, and correcting where appropriate)—and then at some point we look at the entire body of decisions and assess what it all adds up to. The overall structure of thought underlying the decisions that make up the body of laws governing press freedom as conceived in the twentieth century is, I believe, fundamentally sound in its boldness, wisdom, and coherence. But it requires considerable effort and interpretation to locate its basic wisdom and to understand the deeper logic of the decisions. Only by exposing the logic can we reshape and rebuild a jurisprudence suited to new conditions.

The discussion in this chapter is organized around each of the pillars, with some concluding observations on the Court's general strategy and techniques in developing this extremely fertile area of constitutional law.

I

Freedom of speech and press did not expand consistently over the course of the twentieth century. They ebbed and flowed, largely in tandem, with retreat in times of war and national stress and advance in times of relative peace and prosperity. As we have seen, this changed with *New York Times v. Sullivan*, when the country was on the verge of becoming a much more pluralistic society.[1] *Sullivan*'s appealing characterization of the nation's commitment to a public debate that is "uninhibited, robust, and wide-open" wove together the strongest and most eloquent arguments for freedom of speech and press and pushed out the boundary of protection. The question for us is: What was the spirit behind this choice?

It has been customary to locate the rationale for the First Amendment in three general theories, each of which starts from the premise that speech is uniquely good and the source of something valuable. One theory involves the interest of individuals in expressing themselves as a means of fulfilling their basic human potential. For a variety of reasons, this theory has not provided a compelling rationale for the First Amendment. (Speech as a means of self-fulfillment and self-realization can be seen as too ill defined for judges to work with comfortably, indistinguishable from other meaningful human activities, and too disconnected from the pragmatic constitutional concerns of creating a self-governing democracy.) The other two theories have provided working rationales for the First Amendment. The first of these holds that we have an interest in discovering the truth and that the best way to achieve this goal is through a system of largely unregulated discussion. This theory presumes that both individual and society will be better able to arrive at the truth if the government does not limit what can be said. The intellectual roots of this idea go back many centuries to the classic arguments found in John Milton's *Areopagitica* and John Stuart Mill's *On Liberty*. Milton argued that we can trust truth to defeat falsehood.[2] Mill had less faith in truth; he argued that we can never be completely certain that what we believe is true, and therefore a rational person should always want to hear competing ideas.

It was a dissenting opinion by Justice Holmes in 1919 that provided the central articulation of this idea in modern First Amendment jurisprudence. He issued this opinion in a case involving the prosecution and conviction of five Russian immigrants for distributing pamphlets calling for a general strike to protest American military moves thought to be threatening to the Russian Revolution. According to Holmes, it is perfectly logical to want to silence people for expressing opinions contrary to one's own. Any other position would suggest indifference to the ultimate course of events. But there comes a time when people, looking back through history and surveying the wreckage of many "fighting faiths"—including their own—realize that:

> the ultimate good desired is better reached by free trade in ideas—that the best test of truth is the power of the thought to get itself accepted in the competition of the market, and that truth is the only ground upon which their wishes safely can be carried out. That at any rate is the theory of our Constitution. It is an experiment, as all life is an experiment.[3]

The third and most widely embraced rationale for the First Amendment is the one most closely associated with the Court's opinion in *Sullivan*. This is the idea that freedom of speech and press are essential to a self-governing society. Citizens cannot make wise decisions if the government decides that they cannot hear certain ideas.[4] This rationale has had a powerful influence on both the jurisprudence and the popular understanding of what freedom of speech and press means.

These rationales for protecting the freedom of speech and press raise many questions. For example, is commercial advertising sufficiently relevant to truth seeking or self-governance to warrant constitutional protection? What about censorship laws that emerge from the democratic process in which a majority of citizens decides to prohibit the expression of certain ideas? Most censorship in the United States has reflected general public sentiment, but the courts have never taken that into account in deciding whether censorship is permissible. Why is speech, as one form of human behavior among many, exempt from the usual rules of democracy? One might answer that the First Amendment protects "speech" and "press," not eating, jogging, or driving. But, insofar as we want to have sound reasons for our decisions, we ought to look for an explanation beyond the text. Another question is: Why has the freedom of speech and press been taken so far? As we have seen, there are plenty of exceptions to the general rule. Fighting words, obscenity, threats, libel, and the express advocacy of serious illegal action are all subject to regulation in some circumstances. But overall, the Court has interpreted the First Amendment in a way that requires American society to risk a fair amount of harm before the government may intervene.

Extraordinary protection is conventionally justified by invoking the practical dangers of granting the government greater authority to restrict speech. The so-called line-drawing, or slippery slope, problem points to the risks to "good" speech in prohibitions of "bad" speech. There are a number of assumptions behind this argument: Political majorities and government officials cannot be trusted to exercise the power of censorship in a moderate fashion. Intolerance is natural, especially in times of stress. Given the opportunity to censor, people will censor, particularly when they feel anxious or threatened. Moreover, many citizens do not value public debate enough to take the risks involved in guaranteeing freedom for others. Courts cannot always be counted on to stand up to waves of intolerance. Judges fear the psychology of intolerance as it spreads through society the way central bankers fear the mass psychology of inflation. For freedom of speech and press, therefore, it makes sense to push the line of protection far beyond what seems "reasonable" to some.

But there is another, entirely new way of looking at what the Court has been trying to do with the principles of freedom of speech and press. To paraphrase Holmes, it is a great social experiment in tolerance. The point is to shift our focus from seeing the value of speech itself to seeing the need to deal with the problems revealed in the *reactions* to speech. The extraordinary zone of freedom for expression tests our ability to live in a society that is necessarily defined by conflict and controversy; it trains us in the art of tolerance and steels us for its vicissitudes. Consider what Holmes said about "persecution" for expression.[5] It is "logical," as Holmes put it, to feel that we must take action when we encounter ideas that we believe to be wrong. We want to maintain that our beliefs are true and align ourselves with others who share our beliefs. We may fear that, if we do not prohibit bad ideas, we will indicate to others (and to ourselves) that we doubt our own beliefs or lack the courage of our convictions. Add to this the frustration we may feel because we cannot "prove" what we believe to be true, and it is easy to see why people choose suppression over debate, if they can.

There are three points to emphasize here. First, these are responses common to all of us, not just to people who are "bad" and seek to censor. Second, these thoughts and feelings affect all kinds of interactions, not just those involving speech. Third, these reactions can lead to behavior destructive of a pluralistic polity: excessive insistence on the uniformity of majoritarian belief, unwillingness to compromise, undue allegiance to a particular form of social organization, even punitive vindictiveness—all of which are elements leading to an authoritarian regime.

It is easy to say that we should strive to hear other points of view, that we should see the world as others do, or that we should always be ready to change our minds when confronted with arguments we cannot refute. We have all said these things at one time or another, and, of course, they point to a profound—if at times banal—truth about life. But the more interesting and important questions are: Why is this so hard (and even impossible at some level) to do, and what does that reveal about the more fundamental problem of creating a national character—or temperament—capable of resolving conflicts of all kinds? Many great minds over time have recognized the difficulty of controlling the inclinations that produce this authoritarian mindset and have proposed ideas to contain it. John Stuart Mill's famous "harm principle" is one such example. To check the "tyranny of the majority," he argued, there must be a norm that the state cannot interfere with individual liberty until the point where actions cause recognizable harm to others.[6]

Approaching our extraordinary protection of freedom of speech and press as an experiment in tolerance, and avoidance of tyranny, opens up a new way to think about it. We can see the restraint practiced with speech and press not only as a means of protecting something of great and unique value (that is, open discussion), but also as a means of providing experience in moderating natural but dangerous individual and societal tendencies. Through this experiment, we commit ourselves to being, in the language of *Sullivan*, people of "fortitude"[7] who can deal calmly with differences of opinion, scathing dissent, and the risk of disorder—the prelude, as it were, to handling other conflicts that inhere in any truly pluralistic society. We change the valence of tolerance, defining it as a matter of courage rather than weakness and signifying the importance of developing a democratic temperament.

The best way to think of freedom of speech and press, then, is not just as an aid in the search for truth (political and otherwise) but also as creating an unregulated public arena, a special zone of social interaction, where *general* skills and capacities can be highlighted and developed, in the way that being exposed in a wilderness area to the vicissitudes of nature can generate a certain awareness and character needed in a modern, largely urban nation. The press is the most powerful, the most visible, and therefore the most important element of this arena. At its best, the press exposes corruption and incompetence, but it also confronts us with the bewildering complexity of issues, a distressing range of opinions, and the regret that often accompanies difficult decisions. It will always seem simpler in a world of complexity and conflict to retreat into silence and to wield unchallenged power. If we can tolerate freedom of the press, we can learn to tolerate—and even to live successfully in—a free and diverse society. That is the experiment that the great tradition of twentieth-century First Amendment jurisprudence proposes.

II

It may seem odd that the second pillar—the Court's reluctance to embrace a vigorous right to gather news—should have developed as it has. Given the enthusiastic expansion of protection for freedom of the press, and given the critical role the Court has given the press to play in our democracy, we might expect a comparable expansion of the right to gather information. Of course, the cases rejecting that view were often 5–4 decisions. Furthermore, the principal cases involving newsgathering arose under the Burger and Rehnquist courts, rather than the Warren Court, which had earlier created the first pillar. Changes in judicial personnel, combined with a general fatigue about expanding constitutional rights in the 1970s, may be part of the explanation.

But there are significant arguments to be considered against strong protection of newsgathering. One difficulty is knowing where to draw the line if the Court starts down the path of protecting a right of access to those things "needed" for effective reporting. A similar line-drawing problem exists on the speech side of the First Amendment: Does freedom of speech protect only written and verbal language? Or does it also include other behavior that constitutes "expression"? For a long time, this was a conundrum for First Amendment analyses. No one seemed to have an adequate answer. Early on, the Court decided that certain behavior other than "pure" speech should be protected under the First Amendment.[8] The Court protected marches, demonstrations, picketing, flags, expressive armbands, and other forms of behavior by which people conveyed their ideas.[9] But because almost all conduct can be "expressive," there was a need for a limiting principle. Assassination, for example, may be intended to send a political "message," but no sensible person would want to protect assassination as speech.

Finally, in a 1968 case involving a conviction for burning a draft card to protest the military draft, the Court put the issue on an intellectually sound footing. It held that, if the challenged law was directed at "noncommunicative" harms (i.e., at harms having nothing to do with the fact that the defendant's conduct was expressive), it would accord great deference to the judgment of the legislature.[10] For example, a person who paints a message on a public building to express his disapproval of the government can constitutionally be punished for violating a law prohibiting the defacement of public property because the law is not directed at speech but rather at avoiding the costs of cleaning the building. It has only an "incidental" impact on free speech.

This doctrinal development highlights a difficult issue about how much of the landscape the First Amendment should cover. Thinking about this problem helps us to see more vividly the dilemma in asking whether the First Amendment protects all the things we "need" in order to ensure that the rights to free speech and press are "effective." It does not take a great leap of imagination to conclude that a good education is vital to a person's effective freedom of expression. So, too, is a decent income and good health. One can multiply the examples.

By analogy, granting a right of access to information under the control of the government leads to the question: What information? Government is a massive enterprise, and the amount of information under its control is almost beyond comprehension. Consequently, granting such a right could produce a flood of lawsuits pitting the public's right to know against the government's interest in maintaining privacy and secrecy. In addition, there is the issue about who would be classified as the "press" for the purpose of asserting this right. Even members of the press have divided over whether a special right of the press to gather news would undermine the role of the press as an independent institution. "Special privileges" usually come with "special responsibilities." The definitional problem—who constitutes "the press"—has seemed intractable.

Of course, the Court's decisions rejecting a right to gather news happened in a broader societal context. As we have seen, the press in the 1970s was steadily gaining in economic and institutional power in the new role it was assuming in the American democracy.[11] The *Pentagon Papers Case* provided vivid testimony to the status the press had achieved. In the era of Watergate and investigative journalism, the press was emboldened to find new ways of obtaining information and even helped to unseat a president.

The definitive commentary of the time about the good sense in the Court's approach was penned by the constitutional scholar Alexander Bickel: "[G]overnment may guard mightily against… leaks, and yet must suffer them if they occur.… It is a disorderly situation surely. But if we ordered it we would have to sacrifice one of two contending values—privacy or public discourse—which are ultimately irreconcilable."[12] He noted that the *Pentagon Papers Case* "ordains an unruly contest between the press…and government."[13] Here, in essence, is a vision of the era, captured in the doctrines of the First Amendment. On the one side stood the government: necessary for the realization of the public good but prone to abuse of power, to resist public oversight, and to invoke secrecy for the wrong reasons. On the other side stood the press: the public's agent in watching the government and keeping the public informed, but not *too* informed.

In this conception, the Constitution strikes a grand bargain. The extraordinary protection of the free press in the first pillar is what the government has to give up. The lack of a right of newsgathering is what the press gives up in return. It is a contest between equals, which elevates and respects the stature of the press. The government and the press are set in a perpetual state of tension in order to serve the public good. There are rules of engagement, with each side having rights that can be abused. The press has the freedom to say irresponsible and injurious things. The government has the freedom to conduct its business in secret, without any constitutional obligation to disclose information to the press.

III

The third pillar presents a more complicated story. As we have seen, we have created a dual system of the press. On one side stand the print media, with respect to which no public regulations requiring broadened coverage of viewpoints are allowed. On the other side stand the broadcast media, which is largely privately operated but subject to extensive government regulation in the public interest. The Court's rationale for this dual system is premised largely on the "scarcity" of the airwaves.

There are a number of ways of looking at this rationale for the difference in treatment. First, we might see this as the Court presented it: The limited nature of the electromagnetic spectrum justifies the special exception of broadcasting from the norm represented by the print media, and the difference makes sense unless and until circumstances change. Second, we might question the scarcity rationale on the ground that it was premised on a flawed distinction from the beginning. The flaw should be acknowledged, and broadcasting should be brought into the print model.[14] Third, we might conclude that the scarcity rationale is sound, but that the Court has failed to see a parallel scarcity problem with newspapers—a scarcity caused by economic forces rather than physical limitations. In light of these economic realities, the Court should uphold regulations of the print media that are comparable to those it has upheld for the broadcast media.[15]

My own view differs from all of these positions. I agree that the scarcity rationale is analytically unsound. But, in my judgment, the dual system made perfect sense as a reasonable and creative response to a number of important concerns about media generally in the twentieth century. The first was worry about the increasing concentration of ownership and control of the press. One of the most profound social changes of the post–World War II period was that competition among daily newspapers came to an end.[16] It is easy to explain why. Newspapers draw some revenue from subscriptions, but they derive most of their revenue from advertising, both commercial and classified. Advertisers naturally prefer to place their ads in newspapers with the largest circulations, and as people's lives evolved in ways that made the morning papers more appealing, afternoon papers suffered a downward spiral. In addition, it is expensive to start a newspaper. It takes an enormous investment to produce the first copy, though all copies after that are relatively cheap to make. This creates a high barrier to competition from potential entrants. Thus, by the end of the twentieth century, nearly all of the daily newspapers had secured monopolies in their respective communities.[17]

At the same time, daily newspapers were rolled up into chains, such as Gannett, Knight-Ridder, and Hearst. To forestall a potential bottleneck in the flow of information and ideas, various public policies were proposed and some adopted. The nation's antitrust laws were amended to permit newspapers competing in the same market to form "joint operating agreements" when one was at risk of failing.[18] The goal was to reduce costs in business operations while (it was hoped) maintaining separate news and editorial functions. Some cities (e.g., Seattle, San Francisco, Detroit) were able to support two newspapers with this kind of arrangement. Another public policy directed at concentration of the press was the FCC's cross-ownership rule, which prevented newspapers from controlling broadcast stations in the same community.[19]

There was also concern about the growing commercialization of the media. Critics felt that the press was sacrificing journalistic integrity both to avoid offending advertisers and to increase their audiences. The charge was that media outlets were spending too much time and resources on stories that appealed to people's baser impulses and not enough on those that kept them informed. This critique was delivered in many forms, but perhaps the best example was the report of the Hutchins Commission of the late 1940s. The commission was funded by Time, Inc., and Encyclopedia Britannica, Inc., and administered by the University of Chicago. Members included Harold Lasswell (professor of law at Yale), Reinhold Niebuhr (professor of ethics and philosophy at Union Theological Seminary), and Beardsley Ruml (chair of the Federal Reserve Bank of New York); it was chaired by the well-known president of the University of Chicago, Robert M. Hutchins.[20] The Hutchins Report began by noting the contrast between the circumstances governing the press when the country was founded and those at the midpoint of the twentieth century. When the First Amendment was adopted and for many years thereafter, "anybody with anything to say had comparatively little difficulty in getting it published":

> Presses were cheap; the journeyman printer could become a publisher and editor by borrowing the few dollars he needed to set up his shop and by hiring an assistant or two. With a limited number of people who could read, and with property qualifications for the suffrage—less than 6 percent of the adult population voted for the conventions held to ratify the Constitution—there

was no great discrepancy between the number of those who could read and were active citizens and those who could command the financial resources to engage in publication.[21]

Under the circumstances, "in each village and town, with its relatively simple social structure and its wealth of neighborly contacts, various opinions might encounter each other in face-to-face meetings; the truth, it was hoped, would be sorted out by competition in the local market place."[22] But by the time the Hutchins Report was written, "[n]inety two per cent of the communities in this country, all but the bigger cities, have only one local newspaper."[23]

The commission assailed the press for failing to adjust its journalistic standards to accord with the extraordinary power it now wielded. It is remarkable how resonant its indictment remains:

> The news is twisted by the emphasis on firstness, on the novel and sensational; by the personal interests of the owners; and by pressure groups. Too much of the regular output of the press consists of a miscellaneous succession of stories and images which have no relation to the typical lives of real people anywhere. Too often the result is a meaninglessness, flatness, distortion, and the perpetuation of misunderstanding among widely scattered groups whose only contact is through these media.[24]

The "economic logic of private enterprise forces most units of the mass communications industry to seek an ever larger audience," with the result that "[t]he American newspaper is now as much a medium of entertainment, specialized information, and advertising as it is of news." "To attract the maximum audience, the press emphasizes the exceptional rather than the representative, the sensational rather than the significant."[25]

The commission recommended that "the great agencies of mass communications" regard themselves as "common carriers of public discussion." The press must understand that it performs a public service and that "there are some things which a truly professional [journalist] will not do for money."[26] It is interesting to note that, despite the Hutchins Report's critique, between 1977 and 1997, "celebrity, scandal, gossip, and similar stories increased" in network news programs "from 15 percent of the total coverage to 43 percent," according to one study.[27]

Another anxiety traceable throughout the twentieth-century discussions about the American press is the fear that the public is not up to the hard work of self-government. The Hutchins Commission argued that the public did not understand what it needed and how the press was failing it:

> We have the impression that the American people do not realize what has happened to them. They are not aware that the communications revolution has occurred. They do not appreciate the tremendous power which the new instruments and the new organization of the press place in the hands of a few men. They have not yet understood how far the performance of the press falls short of the requirements of a free society in the world today.[28]

All of these concerns—about the concentration of control, about how the free market was distorting journalistic behavior, and about the tendencies among citizens not to live up to their civic responsibilities—were part of the context in which the third pillar was developed.

It is also important to understand the weakness of the rationale for broadcast regulation. The scarcity rationale posited a world in which broadcasting was subject to the "physical" limitations of the electromagnetic spectrum and to the fact that there were more potential users than the spectrum could accommodate. Absent some means of allocating the use of the spectrum, there would be "chaos."[29] It followed, according to the scarcity thesis, that the government had to intervene, allocating the licenses in a way that would serve the public interest and then providing ongoing supervision and regulation to ensure that the new medium met its full potential to inform citizens.[30]

According to the scarcity thesis, broadcasting was an anomaly in our system of the press, distinguishable from all forms of print media, including newspapers. This view was embraced by all sides of the political and jurisprudential spectrum. The print media stood shoulder to shoulder with strong free press advocates to defend the broadcast regulatory regime. Recall that *Red Lion* was a unanimous decision.[31] Even the American Civil Liberties Union argued that regulation was constitutional.[32] Broadcasters themselves seemed tentative about claiming a constitutional status on a par with newspapers.

Things began to change around the time of *Red Lion*. A wing of legal opinion began to see broadcast regulation and especially the Fairness Doctrine as a model for regulating all media, especially daily newspapers. As we saw earlier, that movement was firmly rebuffed by the Court in *Miami Herald v. Tornillo*. Then, in the 1980s, as American society moved politically to the right, some began to challenge the broadcast regulation model as inefficient and constitutionally suspect. By the late 1980s, this attitude led the FCC to jettison the Fairness Doctrine and to loosen some other elements of the regulatory system for broadcasting.[33]

In spite of these swings, the foundations of the dual system have remained in place. But, as early as the 1960s, it had become apparent that the scarcity rationale was inadequate to explain this system.

The primary problem with the scarcity rationale was captured by the simple, yet profound observation that the print media also utilize elements that are "physically scarce." Land, paper, ink, machinery, and all the other things necessary to produce a successful newspaper are also scarce. What is important is not scarcity, but the availability of an alternative to government regulation. That alternative is the market. Instead of regulating the airwaves, the government could simply have conducted an auction, sold off rights to use the spectrum, and then let those who bought the rights treat them as private property, no different from newspapers.[34] The market could then perform its magic of best meeting the preferences of the public—just as it does with newspapers, magazines, and other print media. Indeed, given that this is what we have done with the print media and given our distrust of the government when it comes to manipulating the press, a free market approach would seem to have great advantages.

Some people object that wealth, whether individual or corporate, should not determine who gets control of the airwaves. But the exact same objection could be raised with respect to the print media. All things considered, the critique of the scarcity rationale seems definitive.

But the First Amendment analysis cannot end there. It can be argued that, quite apart from the scarcity rationale, broadcasting is different because the physical limitations are so severe that only a few owners can run the show. In other words, the First Amendment is intended to support a system of speech and press that affirmatively enables multiple voices and views to compete. If there is a bottleneck in the marketplace, which allows a few people or organizations to control public debate, then the government must be able to intervene to correct that situation. Indeed, one might even argue that the First Amendment *requires* the government to take remedial action, as the Court in *Red Lion* at one point intimated.[35]

The most serious problem with the bottleneck thesis is in explaining what constitutes a bottleneck and whether the particular cause of constraint should matter. This leads us back to the observation made earlier about the growing concern in the twentieth century about newspapers effectively becoming natural monopolies in their communities. From a First Amendment perspective, it would seem significant that, at least at the time of *Red Lion*, the average American community had access to only one daily newspaper but three or four VHF television stations and many more radio stations.[36] Determining when the threshold of concentration is crossed is difficult, but it was even more difficult to conclude in the late twentieth century that broadcasting had crossed that threshold but newspapers had not.

But, ironically, there is something about the very weakness of the Court's scarcity rationale that suggests more must be going on. I think the heart of the solution to the paradox of the dual system of freedom of the press that was developed in the twentieth century is a basic ambivalence about what we want to achieve. On the one hand, we want a vigorous marketplace of ideas. We know that a vital press is critical to achieving this. The press can get us the information we need to make the tough decisions we are called on to make in a democratic system. The press can help us to define and shape the national agenda. The press can provide us with the context for evaluating our policies and help us to understand what is happening in our world. To do these things, the press must be large and institutional. It is not easy to provide a check on the government and to stand up to government authority. The larger the scale of the press, the easier it will be for it to serve the public.

On the other hand, we worry that the press will be diverted from its mission in any number of ways, but particularly because of the effects of the market. The market gives feedback to the press about the wants of the public, but it also creates the risk that the hard work of self-governance and public education will be waylaid by baser interests. The press may succumb to the demands of advertisers, its main source of revenue, to avoid controversy or to promote certain positions, and it may follow its own desire to maximize profits at the expense of serious public discourse. Moreover, a powerful institutional press creates risks beyond the potential distortions of the profit motive. The press may advance a one-sided view of important issues; it may become too established, too complacent, or too driven by the ideological interests of those who control it. With large size comes large risk. The press may be a check on the government, but what is the check on the press?

We are thus ambivalent. We want both a powerful and independent press that is free to check the government, and we also want a responsible press that is subject to government regulation. That being so, it becomes entirely reasonable to consider having different, or multiple, alignments or balances when dealing with different technologies of communication. Whether it makes sense to have several systems for the press—some entirely free and unregulated, some regulated according to the public interest, and some sponsored by the government with independent editorial control—should not depend on whether each is materially different from the other. The logic of checks and balances—the essence of our structure of government—is the same logic here. In a world in which no one or no institution can be fully trusted to protect and preserve the public forum we aspire to have, there are many benefits to having multiple approaches. We can learn from practical experience how such systems work but, more important, there are ways in which each part can function as a check on the other. There is nothing in the First Amendment that compels us to have a single, unified system of a free press. New communication technologies, therefore, can offer opportunities to explore these alternative models.

That, it seems to me, is the better account of what really motivated both Congress and the Court as they set about creating our current system. The history of broadcast regulation that otherwise seems inexplicable, even at times a bit bizarre, supports this account. The language used in the cases—*Red Lion* and *Miami Herald* are emblematic—is completely singular for each medium. Each approach is hermetic and insular. In *Red Lion*, the Court never once used the words "journalist" or "press" or "editor" when speaking of broadcasters. Instead, the Court referred to them as "licensees" and "fiduciaries," which could be regulated to protect the public interest.[37] The government, in this vision of the press, was the representative of the people and acted to enforce the right of the people to receive the information and ideas they need to govern. In *Miami Herald*, in contrast, the Court spoke of "journalists," "editors," and the "press." Newspapers must have "journalistic discretion." Here, there was no room in our First Amendment tradition for the government to intervene in the editorial judgments of "editors."[38] (Interestingly, when the Court has confronted questions of government regulation of public broadcasting—the third element in the system of the press—it has followed a line much closer to that governing the print media.)

This way of dealing with each medium as if it were in complete isolation from the others leaves the impression that what lay behind this approach was a sense that it would be desirable to have multiple approaches to the First Amendment, even though the supposedly distinguishing characteristics used to justify the differential treatment were ephemeral.

As we have seen, when cable entered the picture, the Court's analysis faltered because it could not fit the new medium into the broadcast-print dichotomy. Focusing on the number of channels misses the relevant issue, which is not about channels (or pages) but about *control*. To some extent, the debate has slipped into a pointless inquiry into whether monopoly status was caused by physical limits or market dysfunction. Pursuing this analysis might lead to the conclusion that because cable is a natural monopoly, it should be treated like newspapers. But the Court does not seem enthusiastic about posing the issue this way. Instead, it has tended to revert to the simple, and simplistic, conclusion that cable is a medium in flux, and in the end, every medium must be treated on its own merits. This is a weak way of endorsing the most sensible method: that having multiple approaches to the conflicting benefits and risks of a wholly independent press is the best way to achieve our ultimate goal of creating an overall press that is both robust and responsible to the public good.

IV

The press and the principle of freedom of the press evolved over the course of the twentieth century in a historical context in which larger forces were at work transforming and reshaping the way people live and think. The press we need for a changing world also has had to evolve. The First Amendment helped to provide both the framework and the stimulus for that evolution.

Among the many changes that reordered life in America, several were of direct relevance to reshaping the press. One was the shift from a local society to a national one. States and cities ceded authority to the national government in many areas of public life. As the country's challenges became national in scope, responses increasingly could be devised only at the national level. New technologies, especially in transportation and communication, brought closer integration of the society. The expansion of knowledge, especially in the sciences and technology, happened at a pace unseen before in human history. Specialization and expertise magnified the unprecedented accumulation of new insights and reshaped the way people live, while the interconnecting web of general knowledge— upon which we rely to mediate among these specialized areas of knowledge—became simultaneously more important and more difficult to acquire. The nation also became increasingly diverse and pluralistic, especially as previously excluded groups were integrated into the political and social life of the nation.

A press suited to serve in this new environment was needed. As the role of the national government increased, so did the strength and power of the institution of the press, which required a larger scale to report on and to keep watch over the government. From that perspective, the concentration of ownership was a positive development. It allowed the press to accumulate wealth which could be used to increase the staff and the level of expertise of newsrooms. Specialists with extensive educational backgrounds in law, science, economics, the arts, and other fields were hired to report on their respective areas of knowledge. The concentration of power also reinforced a norm of journalism as having a responsibility to provide coverage of different points of view and to be balanced and fair. The institutional press became the primary center of national discussion and debate.

The case of *New York Times v. Sullivan* reflects and symbolizes the interplay of these historical forces. It arose out of the major civil rights movement of the era and was prompted by the Supreme Court's 1954 decision in *Brown v. Board of Education,* which itself challenged a state's right to organize society as it saw fit. The local official's lawsuit and the Alabama court's decision against the *New York Times* were both partly motivated by a determination to resist the nationalization of moral and constitutional norms. The Court's response to this resistance, in turn, symbolized and reaffirmed the necessity for national authority and the commitment to racial and other diversity across American society. *Sullivan* showed, too, that the role of the press was changing. And the Court's refusal to allow Alabama to hold the newspaper legally responsible for the advertisement supported this new role of the press as a forum for public debate as well as a source of news.

The context of local censorship was shifting in two quite opposite ways but with the same upshot of making it untenable. First, as a practical matter, local censorship was often ineffectual in serving local interests. National coverage of a gruesome local murder, for example, rendered impotent a local trial judge's order to the local press not to speak about the case. Second, the nation could no longer tolerate a system of local censorship, because in many cases local censorship would effectively constitute national censorship. In a world in which information needed to flow at a national scale, restrictions at the local level could significantly disrupt the flow of information everywhere. This was true both because local censorship could sometimes prevent information from being known nationally and because local censorship, as in *New York Times v. Sullivan*, could deter national publishers from presenting news that might result in liability in the most restrictive jurisdiction. Publishers would be willing to publish only what would avoid legal liability *everywhere*.

This was what confronted the Court in *New York Times v. Sullivan*. The *New York Times* was gradually becoming the national newspaper for an increasingly nationalized society. The several hundred copies of the *Times* that found their way into Alabama forced the Court to reconsider the historical prerogative of every local jurisdiction to strike its own balance between an interest in an individual's reputation and a free press. This tradition was required to give way in a new era involving an increasingly pluralistic nation with a national press. Thus, *Sullivan* was about much more than just fixing a constitutional standard that would be the fundamental law for every part of the country. It was also about creating the conditions that would allow the new political realities to work.

Television and radio seemed naturally to evolve into national media. The economics of producing content for these media favored their serving the largest possible audience. The national networks were the result of this economic reality. The government and the

Federal Communications Commission, accordingly, felt little need to encourage this development on the theory that it was happening on its own. The concern, instead, was that the missing coverage would be in the area of local affairs. This led to the long-standing regulatory effort to encourage local content.

Throughout this period, the Court employed a certain set of strategies to advance the overarching goal of preserving an extraordinary zone of public discussion—both as a means of yielding better ideas and as a venue in which citizens could develop the capacities of mind and character that are so necessary in an increasingly complex and pluralistic society. The Court took seemingly small human and legal issues and linked the discussions about them to the most profound values defining the nation. It connected the dots of cases about small issues and created a national narrative about a national public forum and its meaning for an ever-changing society. In doing this, it was one of the most vigorous and articulate voices for the role of a free press in American society. If we step back from all that was created over just eight decades of the twentieth century, we can see the development of a highly intricate and elaborate jurisprudential structure that demonstrated the extraordinary commitment of our society to the values of free speech and a free press. Perhaps, most of all, the jurisprudence was characterized by a basic distrust of, and ambivalence about, each major participant (the government, the public, the courts, and the press)—and ambivalence is always at the core of any theory of checks and balances—while aimed at achieving a society dedicated to spirited and informed public debate.

CHAPTER THREE

Regardless of Frontiers

AT THIS MOMENT early in the twenty-first century, it seems appropriate both to try to anticipate where we are likely to go in the decades ahead and to think about where we want to be going. The world in which the free press operates is experiencing tectonic shifts, and these have momentous implications for our understanding of the First Amendment. Some of the forces transforming the press are well known. Some are not. How well we understand these forces, and how well we respond to them, will determine not only the kind of press we will have but also the kind of lives we will live.

The two forces that have most affected both the everyday practices of the press and our sense of what "the press" means are new technologies of communication and globalization. The Internet is enhancing the power and reach of the press even as it weakens traditional media forms, while globalization is creating a new economic and political community. At the same time, though, the fundamental presuppositions that produced our current system of freedom of the press remain largely intact.

I

In some ways, the world has not changed at all. That the jurisprudence of freedom of speech and the press is created in the crucible of war is a very old story. It is when a society feels most threatened that freedom of speech and press matter the most, because it is then that our natural tendency to drift into an authoritarian mindset is most acute. Since the attacks of September 11, 2001, the United States has been at war; the country was plunged into a state of despair, fear, and anger, then mobilized into military action, just as it was during World Wars I and II and the "red scare" of the McCarthy period. For a time, jingoism surged, while dissent became viewed as unpatriotic. Critics of the war in Iraq were accused of betraying the memories of those who had lost their lives in the attacks and of magnifying the risks faced by those asked to serve on the front lines. Ideologues in the media exacerbated those attitudes. The administration of George W. Bush called for a retreat from our commitment to civil liberties.

All of this had a large effect on the press, which, with a few remarkable exceptions, remained (at least in the first few years after 9/11) conspicuously unquestioning about the course the country was on. More recently, there has been a lot of soul searching in the journalism community about why this was so. There is now widespread acknowledgment that the press did not meet its responsibilities during this time.

Another major area of concern during this period involved the relationship between the military and the media regarding the wars in Afghanistan and Iraq. The press has always had to fight to get to the front lines in wartime and to get hold of accurate information. But these wars took the battle between the military and the media to a new level and raised important questions that begin with this: To what extent is the government warranted in deliberately misleading the press—and the public—in wartime? In this particular case, the issue was: Should the United States blur the line between information operations (IO), psychological operations (psyops) and the public affairs office?

Traditionally, there has been a strong division between these military functions. At the National War College, for example, students are offered instruction in information operations. The IO concentration trains students to "apply both information technology and the content it carries in the 'worldwide war of ideas.'"[1] This suggests a very different mission from the traditional relationship of the military to the media. This relationship can be illustrated by the National Defense University course entitled "The News Media," which addresses the constitutional structure underlying the media and the historical development of the relationship between the media and the military, and by the U.S. Military Academy seminar "Mass Media & American Politics," which introduces "cadets to what is perhaps the single most influential private institution in the American political system—oftentimes referred to as the 'fourth branch' or 'fourth estate' of American government" and to "the roles, motivations, and effects of the constitutionally protected media on American political institutions and policy making."[2]

The Bush administration chose to collapse the historic distinction between these two types of government control of information. In a comprehensive account of this policy, Daniel Schulman, a former assistant editor of the *Columbia Journalism Review*, described the tension between the public affairs model and the IO approach: "Public affairs officers view credibility as a responsibility, while information warriors tend to see it as a commodity."[3] The Bush administration was willing to sacrifice the credibility of its public affairs officers in order to use the press as a weapon in its tactical information operations. Tracing the history of the Bush administration's efforts to control press access and to pursue a policy of disinformation is important in understanding some of the modern threats to an effective free press.

Here is a brief chronology of events. On October 7, 2001, the United States began bombing Afghanistan.[4] On October 19, the *New York Times* reported that the National Imagery and Mapping Agency (part of the Department of Defense) had entered into a contract with Space Imaging, Inc., then the only commercial satellite company providing high-resolution images of Afghanistan. The contract was unique because it granted the Pentagon exclusive access to these images, and it allowed the Pentagon to hold onto this right in perpetuity. The press was allowed to purchase images, but only with government approval. The images the media were prevented from seeing were not classified.[5]

On October 21, the *New York Times* reported that the press was being given limited access to troop activities in Afghanistan. No reporters were on the aircraft carrier *Kitty Hawk*, from which helicopters were being launched to fly to Afghanistan. There were no reporters in Oman, where Special Forces and Army Rangers were believed to be based. The Pentagon argued that these restrictions were necessary both for operational security and for the political needs of U.S. allies. However, the *Times* observed that similar pressures were present in the first Persian Gulf war, yet reporters were accorded much freer access.[6]

At a seminar sponsored by the Brookings Institution on November 8, Pentagon officials insisted that reporters would not be allowed access to U.S. troops during the conflict.[7] But nineteen days later, the first reporters were allowed to follow troops into the war. The first media pool was established on December 1, although the restrictions were high: Reporters could not leave the military base and were extremely limited in what they could cover even on the base. Reporters were permitted to stay for only five-day rotations.[8] On December 6, the Pentagon admitted that soldiers had erred when limiting reporter and photographer coverage of a friendly-fire incident at a military base outside Kandahar by locking the reporters in a warehouse while the wounded and deceased soldiers were returned to the base (even though their families had been notified).[9] On December 13, the Pentagon announced a plan to open three "coalition press information centers," although few if any were near military activity.[10]

In February 2002, in another conflict between the government and the press over access, a *Washington Post* reporter, Doug Struck, traveled to Zhawar, Afghanistan, to investigate whether a Hellfire missile intended to hit Al Qaeda operatives actually killed civilians. As he approached the area, Struck reported, he was held at gunpoint by U.S. soldiers who called their superiors before telling him that he "would be shot" if he proceeded. The Associated Press reported, "Rear Admiral Craig Quigley said the soldiers' words to Struck were: 'For your own safety, we cannot let you go forward. You could be shot in a firefight.'" The assistant secretary of defense for public affairs, Victoria Clarke, attributed the incident in part to the chaos and uncertainty of the battlefield in Afghanistan where, days before the 9/11 attacks, assassinations had been carried out by two men posing as journalists.[11]

At the same time, back in Washington, D.C., a major controversy erupted when it was revealed that the Pentagon was in the process of establishing the Office of Strategic Influence. On February 19, 2002, the *New York Times* published an article (based on a Pentagon leak from a senior official) that first exposed the OSI. The purpose of OSI purportedly went beyond the coordination of the preexisting offices engaged in information operations in the post–9/11 environment. Its mission was to "win hearts and minds" in hostile nations (e.g., Afghanistan) and also to employ similar tactics in allied nations in the Middle East and Western Europe. These efforts would include the deliberate use of misinformation when it was deemed appropriate.[12] On February 26, President Bush expressed his objection to the proposed office, and one day later Secretary Donald Rumsfeld announced that the office would be closed. Rumsfeld subsequently tried to reassure reporters that OSI was not intended to mislead Americans.[13] Several months later, in November, Rumsfeld reasserted his commitment to robust IO, saying, "You can have the name [OSI], but I'm gonna keep doing every single thing that needs to be done, and I have."[14] There were subsequent press reports about how the intentions and methods behind OSI were continued in new forms even after it was formally abandoned.[15]

This shift was also reflected by changes in the chain of command and the integration of public affairs and psyops into the Orwellian-named Office of Theaterwide Interagency Effects. However, these offices were separated in January 2005 in apparent response to a letter from the then-chair of the Joint Chiefs of Staff, General Richard Meyers, which was distributed in the fall of 2004 and expressed concerns about "organization constructs [that] have the potential to compromise the commander's credibility with the media and the public."[16]

With respect to foreign media, though, and the emergent press in Iraq in particular, there was far less regard for the line between public affairs and psyops. One example of this involved the Lincoln Group, a private company hired by the Pentagon in 2005 to do "public relations" work in Iraq. Working in the Information Operations Task Force, the Lincoln Group placed unattributed U.S. propaganda in mainstream Iraqi news sources, either by directly paying the news outlets or by paying an advertising agency. It also paid Iraqi journalists to publish articles that were sympathetic to the U.S. perspective.[17] An investigation in March 2006 ordered by General George W. Casey Jr., the commanding general of Multi-National Force–Iraq, found that the Lincoln Group's actions were not in violation of military policy.[18] Activities like those of the

Lincoln Group were, indeed, not uncommon as part of the psyops campaign.

These policies and practices did not go unchallenged. The State Department's Future of Iraq Project, which included a "free media working group," issued a report in 2002 warning specifically against using the Iraqi press as a propaganda platform. "New forms of propaganda are totally out of the question, even with the best of intentions," the project's working group argued.[19] Even within the military itself, there was substantial concern about the direction taken by psyops with respect to Iraqi and other foreign media.[20]

It should be emphasized that the Pentagon did not view the psyops program as marginal to military efforts and goals. In a speech delivered at the Council on Foreign Relations, Secretary Rumsfeld argued that "some of the most critical battles may not be in the mountains of Afghanistan or the streets of Iraq, but in newsrooms—in places like New York, London, Cairo, and elsewhere." He also emphasized that terrorist organizations themselves realize the importance of the media. According to Rumsfeld, Osama bin Laden's chief lieutenant, Ayman al-Zawahiri, said that "more than half of this battle is taking place in the battlefield of the media.... We are in a media battle in a race for the hearts and minds of [Muslims]."[21]

It is worth noting here in the context of U.S. propaganda efforts in foreign venues that a key part of the structure of U.S. law involves the Smith-Mundt Act of 1948, which authorizes the secretary of state to disseminate abroad "information about the United States, its people, and its policies, through press, publications, radio, motion pictures, and other information media, and through information centers and instructors abroad" but also provides that this "information...shall not be disseminated within the United States."[22] The purpose of the act is to permit propaganda abroad but prohibit the government from using it domestically. For many years, people have questioned whether this limitation can actually work in practice, since information disseminated abroad may very well find its way back into the American media. And, with the Internet, the distinction is even less meaningful in reality. Nevertheless, this remains the operative structure.

Moreover, policies and proposals like the Office of Strategic Influence, and other government-sponsored disinformation activities, raise profound issues not only with respect to their incompatibility with the First Amendment here at home, but also with their impairment of important efforts to establish an independent press in these same countries (efforts that may well be funded by U.S. agencies such as the Agency for International Development).[23] Even if the "bad" information does not make its way back into American newspapers and television broadcasts, it may still harm nascent journalism in societies we care about fostering.[24]

Another flashpoint between the military and the press in Iraq has involved detentions of Iraqi reporters working for the U.S. press (and other foreign news organizations), sometimes for extended periods of time. The most widely reported and discussed involved Bilal Hussein, an Associated Press photographer who contributed to the AP's 2005 Pulitzer Prize–winning photography portfolio. Hussein was arrested in April 2006, alleged to have committed a number of crimes associated with the insurgency. The AP conducted its own investigation and found insufficient evidence to support the charges. Hussein was held for more than twenty months without a formal hearing, and after being detained for two years, all legal proceedings against him were dropped and he was released.[25]

The AP strongly objected to Hussein's arrest and detention. Almost exactly one year after the arrest, Tom Curley, the CEO and president of the Associated Press, argued in a panel on war coverage in New York that the real issue was not Hussein but interference with freedom of the press: "This is not about Bilal Hussein. He's an unfortunate victim. This is about the Associated Press. We are the target. Freedom of the press is the target." Curley added that the military in al-Anbar Province had engaged in "an extreme effort to shut down the coverage in an out-of-control place. That's what this is about."[26] After a closed hearing in December 2007, the Iraqi judicial panel dismissed the allegations against Hussein and ordered his release. The United States finally released Hussein on April 16, 2008.

The Hussein case was only one of several involving the arrest and detention of journalists working in Iraq. The Committee to Protect Journalists has documented numerous instances, supporting the claims of many in the press that the U.S. military freely used this technique to stop or punish press coverage it did not like.[27] There is a larger issue, which concerns the appropriate processes to be followed in such cases. No one, of course, would argue that members of the press are always innocent or may never be arrested or investigated. But there ought to be regularized and timely methods for resolving accusations. Although the military itself has said that the detention of reporters should be reviewed within thirty-six hours,[28] the United States did not follow its own procedures, which led to cases like Hussein's in which the detention extended for years.

The Bush administration further contributed to the culture of hostility in the government toward the press with its policies on issuing subpoenas to reporters. A study in 2008 found a dramatic rise in the number of federal subpoenas issued to the media per year since 2001; the survey reported 74 federal media subpoenas in 2001 and 335 in 2006, 34 of which requested confidential information.[29] Such actions were a breach of an implied understanding with the press that it would be "responsive" to the government when it received classified information in return for the government refraining from issuing subpoenas to reporters unless it were absolutely critical to a criminal investigation.[30]

The litany of conflicts between the Bush administration's Department of Defense and the media over the role of the press in covering the wars in Afghanistan and Iraq is long and serious. From the beginning, the press objected to the delay in activation of pool coverage of combat operations, the efforts to prevent reporters from getting on the ground, the requirements that journalists rely on briefings and leaks for information, the efforts to bar reporters from publishing certain material (e.g., Osama bin Laden tapes), the rules preventing photographers from transmitting some images (e.g., of chained and masked prisoners), and the decisions ending pool coverage and replacing it with "information centers" located away from military activity.[31]

Although several lawsuits by the press were filed during this period over some of these practices, all were quickly dismissed as not involving a First Amendment right (or on grounds of mootness), and none reached the Supreme Court.[32]

II

The Internet is having profound effects on our ability to communicate. Like every major advance in communications technology in the past—including the invention of the Gutenberg press, which first made possible the mechanical replication of pamphlets and books; the system of the rotary press and movable type; the telegraph and telephone; radio and television; and cable and then satellite transmission—the Internet has facilitated a massive expansion in human communication and understanding. It is now possible for millions of people to speak with one another virtually instantaneously from all parts of the planet. Access to knowledge is being equalized beyond anything previously imaginable. And all of this is happening at a cost to the user that can seem negligible. The Internet and all of its associated means of communicating are becoming the primary infrastructure of a global public forum.

The numbers are already impressive. As of March 2009, over 20 percent (approximately 1.5 billion people) of the world's population use the Internet, a more than threefold increase since the mid-1990s.[33] In June 2008 China exceeded the number of Internet users in the United States.[34]

At the same time that the Internet is helping to create a global public forum, other forces are dramatically expanding our interconnectedness and interdependency. There are multiple causes of the process of globalization. Technological advances are certainly important—not only to communication but also to transportation and production. National policies are critical—particularly the greater openness of borders for trade and migration and, most important, the embrace of free markets throughout the world. The spread of common languages, including English, Spanish, and Mandarin, facilitates increased interaction. (Fully a quarter of the world's population now speaks English.)[35]

The world is becoming more integrated, moving inexorably (or so it would seem) toward becoming a single society. One can point to many signs of this. If one looks at the investments from the United States into the rest of the world and from the world into the United States, the data convey vividly the ever-growing entanglement. In the five-year period from 2002 to 2007, global direct investment abroad from the United States rose 233 percent, from $135 billion to $314 billion, while foreign direct investment (FDI) in the United States increased by 311 percent from $75 billion to $233 billion.[36] The year 2007 set a record for FDI among the thirty countries belonging to the Organisation for Economic Co-operation and

Development (OECD), an international group of governments committed to democracy and a market economy.[37] From 2006 to 2007, the FDI outflows from OECD countries increased by over 50 percent, from $1.2 trillion to $1.8 trillion. At the same time, economic power is diffusing. For example, the so-called Group of Seven (G-7), which included those countries that have "traditionally taken the lead in tackling global crises," has declined in international economic power: "Between 1965 and 2002, it accounted for a remarkably constant share of global output—about 65 percent.... By 2030, it is likely to be down to 37 percent." As superpowers decline in economic weight, "the flip side of the coin is the rise of emerging markets."[38] And now the G-7 has become the G-20.

The upshot of this kind of mutual involvement is increased interdependency. Not too long ago, people in one part of the planet could act without significant consequences for people in other parts. That is no longer true, and the examples (good and bad) are legion. The financial crisis and deep recession of 2008–2009 painfully confirmed the reality of economic interdependence. Meanwhile, the world's resources are increasingly stressed, as hundreds of millions of people are able to lead safer, healthier, and more prosperous lives. The degradation of the earth and its atmosphere— most strikingly represented in the reality of global warming—has put us on a path to disaster. International airport arrivals reached 903 million in 2007,[39] with a projected increase to 1.6 billion by 2020.[40] As a result, disease moves freely around the planet. Students, too, are increasingly moving across international borders. The Institute of International Education found a 150 percent increase in the number of Americans studying abroad between 1997 and 2007.[41] Although Europe remains the most popular destination, more students are exploring other parts of the world.[42] Meanwhile, global climate change is increasing desertification, and westward winds take the sands of the Gobi desert and transport dust particles to the west coast of the United States,[43] which may be linked to increases in asthma in the region.[44] There are innumerable similar examples of the shrinking, or flattening, of the world.

But globalization is transforming us in ways other than through the exchange of goods and services or the creation of global problems requiring global solutions. In small and large ways, our outlook on life is changing too. We now know when the Asian stock markets open, and our sense of moral and ethical responsibility is steadily being enlarged as we become more acutely aware of human suffering, such as extreme poverty and deaths from easily preventable diseases, in other parts of the world.

It is also now becoming painfully clear that humanity's existing political institutions for taking collective international action are sadly lagging behind the intricate global interconnections—economic and otherwise—that are being woven. Despite the many successes of our post–World War II global institutions—the United Nations, in particular—we remain far too much a world of independent states, each left to its own devices, despite a need for coordinated action to deal with the mutual dependency of an increasingly global society. The primary model of dealing with our global issues involves continuous negotiations rather than collective governance, except in a few discrete areas such as international trade. This has become even more apparent as the world tries urgently to find the means to climb out of a severe recession and to create a new system of global financial regulation.

The first step in dealing with the daunting issues posed by globalization is to acquire information and knowledge, and this is the primary function of journalism and the press. There are, of course, other institutions whose role it is to nurture our abilities to understand what is happening in the world and how to think about it. Universities, along with the press, are designed to serve that purpose. For a variety of reasons, however, American colleges and universities, as great as they are, also need to reshape their intellectual agendas to accord with the extraordinary march of globalization. This poses interesting and important questions beyond the scope of this volume, but it may be said that the deficit in U.S. higher education with regard to the study of globalization stems from two primary causes. One is that universities by nature are slow-moving institutions, and the forces of globalization have advanced quickly, leaving higher education in a position of having to catch up. The other is that academic inquiry typically moves through cycles of greater and lesser engagement with real world events. There is always some degree of detachment with academic inquiry, given that one of its functions is to think more deeply and systematically about issues than do other institutions. But there are degrees of detachment, and in the last few decades, especially in the social sciences and to some degree in professional fields such as law, there has been a distinct shift toward issues that are more abstract and more removed from actual events. A concrete illustration of this trend has been the marked decline at many leading universities of expertise in societies such as contemporary China, as compared to the expertise of this kind developed in the first quarter century after World War II. To be sure, American universities appreciate their current intellectual deficit, but, as I have mentioned, academic institutions move slowly.

The press and universities have a lot in common—not least, a deep sense of mission in advancing our understanding and knowledge of the world. Together, they provide society with both analysis and information that are, on the one hand, deep and reflective and, on the other, immediate and engaged. Journalism is on the front line of what is happening now. This requires special skills and capacities. Given the rapid changes in the world due to globalization, where we have far less understanding than we need, and given the insufficiency of both political and academic institutions to deal well with what is happening, the press and journalism should take on a greater-than-usual role in helping us to figure out what issues we need to address. This is not, by any means, a minor matter. Take the subject of genocide. The massive slaughters that took place in both Rwanda and Kosovo were not sufficiently attended to by our political institutions, whether national or international. Nor were they sufficiently covered by the media, which may well have contributed to the political failure to stop the horrific killings. Action comes from information, from knowing what is going on. That is the proper province of the press.

Here, however, we confront a conundrum arising out of the very structure of this new world we are entering. The Internet offers the press the opportunity to increase its audience—indeed, to obtain a global audience instantaneously. The four major U.S. newspapers, the *Wall Street Journal,* the *New York Times,* the *Los Angeles Times,* and the *Washington Post,* each have a daily circulation ranging from nearly 700,000 to over 2 million.[45] But their Web sites now attract audiences in the tens of millions (58 million per month in the case of the *New York Times*).[46] Kathleen Carroll, Executive Editor of the Associated Press, told me that, while the AP reaches millions of people daily through newspapers, when you include the Internet as well as other media, AP content connects with half of the world's population daily. Besides an expanded audience, the Internet brings other advantages to the traditional press, including the ability to tell stories using different formats and methods (video, podcast, etc.) and the opportunity to hear back from and to have a dialogue with readers and viewers, while dispensing with the costs of paper and distribution.

But the extraordinary proliferation of voices on the Internet has also led to a dispiriting and sharp decline in the traditional media's audience share and, even more alarmingly, in their advertising revenues, both classified and commercial, which had been the principal financial base for American private media.[47] The migration of classified advertising to the Web has been swift and unrelenting, and general business advertising has also moved, though less precipitously, to the Internet. Although the traditional press's Web sites have enjoyed large audiences, which attract advertisers at much lower rates, this is also true for the countless nonpress Web sites, giving advertisers far more choices and the press far less revenue. (Changes in the nature of audience receptivity to ads also play a role.) Furthermore, except for a small group that specializes in financial news, newspapers have not found a workable means of charging readers for access to their Web sites.[48] This means that the press finds itself in the uncomfortable and unsustainable position of charging customers for the print version while giving it away free on the Internet. The simple fact is that the Internet is undermining the business model of the traditional press.

Just to add some anecdotal detail to this picture, Rupert Murdoch estimated that in the first five or six months of 2008, newspaper revenues in the United States were down "10 to 30 percent."[49] In June 2008, the *Washington Post* reduced its staff by 15 percent.[50] In 2008, newspapers in the United States suffered "a double-digit drop in advertising revenue, raising serious questions about the survival of some papers."[51] The *Philadelphia Inquirer* declared Chapter 11 bankruptcy in February 2009.[52] The *New York Times* announced a first-quarter loss of $74.5 million in April 2009.[53] In just two years, the financial situation of newspapers deteriorated faster than almost anyone had anticipated.

For broadcast networks, there has been similar downward financial pressure. In 2008, the *New York Times* observed that "broadcast television as a medium is in decline because new platforms—the Internet, mobile devices—are fragmenting audiences." The previous year, the three major broadcast news networks averaged a 5 percent decline in viewership, with CBS sustaining a 13 percent loss.[54]

The consequences of this state of affairs for journalism have been dire. Several news organizations have closed altogether, and many more are on the brink of closure. When decisions are taken short of closing, they typically involve cutbacks with significant impact on the flow of news. Often, the number of pages devoted to news is limited, and staff positions are cut. In 2008, the *Los Angeles Times,* which for decades was one of the best papers in the country, eliminated 150 newsroom jobs, which represents over one-sixth of the staff.[55] Layoffs in the media industry became so common by 2008 that a feed on Twitter—the micro-blogging platform—called "The Media Is Dying" was created to alert subscribers to firings in the industry.[56]

In the face of budget crises and staff cuts, one of the first things to go is remote news operations, particularly foreign bureaus and correspondents. The closing of foreign bureaus has been under way for some time now. The significance of this general inattention can be striking. Only the *New York Times* and CNN had journalists in Afghanistan on September 11, 2001; by the summer of 2009, only the *New York Times* and the *Washington Post* have full-time news teams in Afghanistan and Pakistan. Local newspapers that once devoted 10 percent of their columns to international news are now down to only 2 percent.[57] Between 2002 and 2006, the number of foreign-based newspaper correspondents declined by 30 percent.[58] Since the beginning of the war in Iraq, two-thirds of the U.S. newspapers and newspaper chains that maintained full-time bureaus in Baghdad have shuttered them. Most of the American press now relies on the news services Associated Press and Reuters for international news.[59]

Nor has television and radio journalism been exempt from the cuts. Since the late 1980s, ABC has slashed its foreign bureaus by 64 percent. Neither CBS nor NBC has a single full-time correspondent in Iraq.[60] This decrease in foreign bureaus is bound to translate over time into less sophisticated reporting about global matters. What will be lost is the special knowledge that comes from a continuous presence in other regions of the world. There will be an increasing tendency to cover crises rather than presenting the public with what it should know on a more regular basis.

The decline in coverage of global issues is confirmed by a 2008 study conducted by the Pew Research Center for the People and the Press. The study found that "[a]lmost two-thirds of American newspapers publish less foreign news than they did just three years ago," and only 10 percent of newspaper editors "considered foreign news 'very essential' to their papers."[61] Indeed, the amount of pages devoted to news overall has been cut significantly in order to save money.

There is a symbiotic relationship between audience interest and press coverage. When the amount of international news declines, so does interest. The Pew Research Center has found that, although "most Americans continue to track local and national news," most now "follow international news only when important developments occur."[62]

What this all adds up to is a potentially tragic irony: At the moment when our technological capacities to communicate globally are greater than ever, when the interdependency of peoples around the globe is greater than ever, and when the need for news about international and global issues is greater than ever, the technology that facilitates this communication is undermining the capacity of American media institutions to meet their responsibility to the public. America is at risk of intellectual isolationism, at least as grave a problem for the nation as economic protectionism.

It may be said, with some justification, that the Internet is also making it possible for many hundreds and thousands of individuals, groups, and institutions to provide the information that the traditional press can no longer provide. But it is not wise to expect that the gap in our knowledge about what is happening in the world will be filled by these emerging voices on the Internet. It is—and for the foreseeable future will be—the traditional media upon which we must rely for the information we need to fulfill our responsibilities as citizens and as members of the world community.

This is a fitting moment at which to return to a larger perspective on the role of the American press as a center for public information. Nothing compares with the pervasive presence and impact of the press. Newspaper readership in the United States reaches approximately 100 million people daily.[63] Sunday newspaper circulation exceeds 130 million readers. A study of newspaper readership found that "85 percent of Americans still read a newspaper in an average week."[64] Network newscasts, despite declining in influence in recent years, continue to reach 20–30 million people every day.[65] In fall 2008, National Public Radio programming reached 27.5 million listeners weekly, which represents a 7 percent growth from the previous year.[66] The Associated Press maintains a robust international presence, with 3,000 reporters[67] working in over 97 countries in 240 worldwide bureaus,[68] bringing the news to billions of people.[69]

At this moment, we cannot say whether the press as we know it will survive, or whether it will dissolve over time into a plethora of tiny voices still collectively reaching the multitudes. For now, however, we can say this: The press has never before had a greater capacity to speak to the public about what is happening in the world, nor a greater responsibility to help the public understand this reality. Yet this very capacity is undercutting the press's ability to meet its responsibility. The press remains the best option we have for fulfilling the critical role of helping us to engage in collective self-governance. The question is: What can be done to align the press's newfound technological reach with our needs?

III

It is impossible to predict whether this current march toward a global society will continue, or whether—like the last great period of "globalization," which resulted from increased trade at the turn of the twentieth century—it will be felled by regional and world wars leading to self-isolation and economic protectionism. Much depends on the choices we make. One of our choices will be whether to support a free and independent press in its endeavor to provide the world with the information and knowledge necessary to make wise decisions.

Supporting a free press is especially important because we are starting from a combined deficit in our governance and intellectual institutions. By training, experience, and professional disposition, the press is more agile, quicker to see the story, and better able to explain it to the public than any other institution. In the new frontier of globalization, which is still in a primitive state of social organization, the press must be our scout and our explorer. But what does it mean to have a global free press for a global society? The discussion that follows refers to dates and events from a particular slice of time, but the general story is more or less the same over much longer periods.

Let's start with how the press fares in gaining access to the news. Much of the world is simply closed off to reporters. It can be dangerous to enter certain regions, especially where there is civil war or other forms of violence. Moreover, many nations exert strict controls over journalists. Many governments close off their societies in times of perceived crisis or grant access to only favored media. Even in Israel, a society with its own vibrant tradition of free press, public dissent, and independent judiciary, during its assault on Gaza in 2008–2009, its Defense Forces forbade journalists to enter the war zone, while Hamas allowed the Al Jazeera news agency to report on the effects of the bombing.[70] When a devastating cyclone struck

Myanmar in 2008, the ruling junta refused to allow foreign journalists into the country, while it exercised complete control over the country's internal media. As a result, Myanmar's people were left in even more desperate straits.[71]

The practice of cutting off the outside world's access is usually accompanied by seizing control of the press inside the country, with a more or less total lockdown of the society. Naturally, dictatorships are especially prone to such practices. When President Robert Mugabe of Zimbabwe refused to recognize the results of a presidential election, he arrested members of the press who reported in ways that his government disliked.[72] Likewise, in Pakistan, when a crisis erupted over the legitimacy of President Pervez Musharraf's rule, Musharraf implemented an emergency decree under which independent television networks were seized and allowed to continue broadcasting only after agreeing not to report anything "deemed to defame or ridicule the head of state or the army."[73] As I complete this book, Iran is in a state of crisis with protests over its most recent election, in which the current president, Mahmoud Ahmadinejad, dubiously claimed a landslide victory. As the government faces rising opposition among its citizenry, the regime is deploying the standard array of censorship techniques: limiting and revoking visas for foreign journalists; restricting journalists to their hotels and barring them from covering or being present at demonstrations and protests; requiring independent media to submit news reports for official clearance; having reporters detained, arrested, threatened and beaten; blocking websites and monitoring Internet communications; publishing and distributing disinformation; and jamming broadcast signals, especially those coming into the country via satellite (such as the new BBC World Service Persian channel and Radio Farda, the Persian language broadcast and Internet service of Radio Free Europe).[74]

In other countries, the standard procedures for journalistic access can seriously hamper coverage. In China, for example, foreign journalists may be granted permission to report from within the country, but they face many restrictions, including the requirement that they always be accompanied by Chinese nationals. Chinese journalists are taught in school about the reporter's expected role through the concept of "Marxist journalism."[75] And China does not permit foreign journalists to travel to restricted areas without special permission, such as Tibet.[76]

Sending information to a country can be equally vexing. Most developed countries permit foreign print publications to be freely distributed. But there are often constraints. Many countries impose tariffs on foreign publications, some limit distribution to major airports and hotels where foreigners stay, some permit distribution only in kiosks in major cities. China allows U.S. magazines to be circulated in cities, but censors rip out pages with undesirable news or impose bureaucratic licensing rules.[77]

Use of the airwaves is universally regarded as a matter of government prerogative that is usually (certainly in the case of television signals) allocated only, or primarily, to state-approved entities. Canada has a variety of regulations aimed at increasing the Canadian content of media broadcasts,[78] and the European Union requires European stations to commit a majority of their time to European broadcasts.[79] Despite the great advances in free trade, the openness to the exchange of goods and services has not been matched by an openness to the exchange of information and ideas. The World Trade Organization (WTO) agreements governing free trade typically reserve for each country control over certain media, such as film and television broadcasts.[80] International trade negotiations, generally speaking, have not focused on increasing the flow of information nor, for that matter, on developing an independent press as a necessary corollary to developing a free market.

But individual countries may choose to become more open to foreign media. In 2008, India changed its policy to allow "foreign current affairs magazines to print local editions in the country."[81] This means that "magazines such as *Newsweek, BusinessWeek* and *The Economist* can launch Indian editions supported by local advertising without restriction[s] on content." However, "curbs on ownership remain, with foreign media companies limited to stakes of no more than 26 percent in Indian publishing ventures." The Ministry of Information and Broadcasting said that the new policies would "help Indians better understand global events and make foreign news more affordable."[82] The new policy does not cover newspapers.

Of course, both satellite and Internet advances have greatly increased the technological capacity to communicate around the world. There is a natural, and understandable, fascination with the ways in which new communications technologies can enhance expression and affect our lives and world events. During the protests following the 2009 presidential election in Iran, Western news media frequently reported on the use of cell phones and social networking sites as means of facilitating political organization and of getting on-the-ground information out to the world and beyond the grasp of the official censors. But this flow of information (which, while certainly valuable in its own right, can never replace quality news reporting over long periods of time) is neither perfect nor guaranteed. Apart from problems of knowing the context and the authenticity of these communications, governments bent on control-ling the flow of information are unfortunately not defenseless.[83] While censorship is difficult, it is a myth that the Internet makes, or will make, all control impossible. Bandwidth under the control of the state (as the Internet Service Provider) can be severed or reduced, making video traffic and e-mail communication impossible or difficult. The Internet typically enters a country at particular physical points, or gateways, where monitoring and censorship can take place. China, for example, employs thousands of people to check on and block Internet-delivered information at the two gateway points leading into the country (the so-called Great Firewall of China). Gaining access to particular Web sites or information via the Internet can be criminally punished, and high-profile cases of such punishment induce self-censorship.[84] New technologies, such as the so-called deep packet inspection, (employed by Iran) make it possible for governments to monitor online communication on a vast scale. Moreover, when companies, such as Google and Yahoo, set up operations within countries, they typically agree to be bound by local laws, including censorship restrictions and laws and policies requiring the disclosure of information about users that may be used to censor and punish others (making the search engine companies unhappy allies of government censors).[85] Recently, the Chinese government ordered Google to restrict access to certain websites and further announced a requirement that computers imported into the country be equipped with filters, which would facilitate censorship of political expression, though it later backed down from that requirement (a matter we will return to in the next chapter).[86]

Satellite dishes are prohibited in many countries, such as China (except in upscale hotels and foreign compounds) and Iran, although the enforcement is uneven. Moreover, satellite signals can be blocked. My wife and I were in China just as protests erupted in Tibet in 2008. As coverage of these events appeared on the BBC and CNN, the screen suddenly would go dark. On the eve of the twentieth anniversary of the crushing of the pro-democracy movement in Tiananmen Square in 1989, China blocked access to Web sites and BBC World News reports about the anniversary and removed pages in the *International Herald Tribune* that contained an article on the Dalai Lama.[87]

Just to give some flavor to how complicated the world is in this regard, consider the BBC World Service, which has six transmitters in Singapore and Thailand beaming signals into China. China has six transmitters just inside its border to block these signals.[88] (Interestingly, the English shortwave broadcasts, which cover all of China, have not been jammed, but the Mandarin shortwave broadcasts have been since 1989, according to the BBC.)[89] The censorship is inconsistent, but as is usually true with censorship, the goal is to be menacing and to chill speech, rather than to obliterate it entirely.

In fact, we are just at the beginning of a clash of philosophies about the structure of societies and the global society and, in particular, about the nature of expression in the world community. As we have seen, it is easier to get the world to commit itself to free trade in goods and services than to agree on how open our minds should be to competing ideas. There are many different views about the proper role of the press in a society. At one end is the outlook of the United States, which developed, as we've seen, in the twentieth century and which seeks to sustain a vibrant press that facilitates an extrordinarily open system of expression. But many societies see the press differently, as an institution properly aligned with and serving the ends of the government, which itself is responsible for determining what best furthers the well-being of the nation. The press, from this perspective, is merely a means of implementing government policy. In many, if not all, of these countries, the press is either owned by the state or directly subservient to a government ministry charged with oversight of the media. When Vladimir Putin came into power in Russia, one of the first things he did was to end the independence of television stations.[90]

Russia is also notorious for seemingly tolerating (and possibly doing more to encourage) private violence against independent journalists as a surrogate for official censorship. Since Putin became president in 2000, sixteen journalists have been murdered, with only one conviction.[91] The most well known of these is the apparent contract murder of Anna Politkovskaya, who was famous for her reporting on Chechnya, where she covered human rights abuses committed by the Russian military and Chechen rebels. She wrote several award-winning books on the subject and received the Amnesty International Global Award for Human Rights Journalism in 2001. At the time of her murder in 2006, she was writing a column for the biweekly newspaper *Novaya Gazeta,* one of the only major news organizations willing to criticize Putin and the Russian state. Four of its journalists have mysteriously died since 2000.[92]

There are, unfortunately, many other instances of violence against those who disseminate material deemed to be dangerous or offensive. One of the most notorious involved the violence and threats of violence following the publication in a Danish newspaper (*Jyllands-Posten*) of a cartoon with images of Muhammad, implying that the Muslim faith was being used to promote terrorism.[93] In December 2004, a Danish filmmaker, Theo van Gogh, was murdered for perceived anti-Islamic statements.[94] One of the most famous fatwas came from Iranian religious leaders in 1989, who urged that the novelist Salman Rushdie be killed for his novel *The Satanic Verses.*[95]

Violence against journalists and the press is particularly serious in Latin America. One of the prizes for journalism awarded by Columbia University, through the Graduate School of Journalism, is the Maria Moors Cabot Prize honoring journalists who have bravely covered challenging topics in the Americas. The awards ceremony is always moving because it highlights how dangerous it is for journalists to function and how courageous so many are in continuing to report the news in threatening environments. Journalists working in Latin America face a variety of threats, such as governments that imprison journalists on criminal libel charges and criminal gangs and corrupt law enforcement officials who assault, abduct, and murder journalists, too often with impunity because local police or judges are beholden to criminals. As of mid-2009, nowhere in the Americas was it more dangerous to practice journalism than in Mexico. Mexican journalists have been under assault from organized drug gangs that have been gaining control of portions of Mexico, especially along its border with the United States. These criminals have killed and bribed their way into control of the local police and governments and have silenced the press in the process. Twenty-one journalists were killed in Mexico between 2000 and 2008, seven in direct reprisal for their work.[96] Many journalists along the border and in provincial areas of Mexico have been cowed into self-censorship by years of grenade attacks on newsrooms, strafing by automatic weapons fire, abductions, and outright murder.

Censorship laws vary across countries. It is common, even in countries characterized by some elements of democracy, to find restrictions on speech that is deemed to undermine the state, contribute to instability, embarrass the government, or defame the reputation of the state. In China, for instance, there is great alarm over any expression that would encourage protest in rural areas. Turkey forbids speech that constitutes an insult to "Turkishness."[97] In January 2009, an Australian writer was sentenced to three years in prison by a court in Thailand for "insulting the Thai monarchy in a self-published novel," which sold only ten copies. The case was brought under the country's *lèse-majesté* laws, which call for criminal punishments for insulting members of the royal family.[98] These are classic laws against sedition, which the Supreme Court in *New York Times v. Sullivan* said violated the "central meaning" of the First Amendment.

Many nations close to the United States in their forms of government and respect for civil liberties draw different lines when it comes to press freedom. Britain, for instance, has been much more concerned with preserving the sanctity of a fair trial by prohibiting media commentary. It has also had a strict policy against the press publishing state secrets and has favored protections for personal reputation that have made it easier for plaintiffs to recover damages for libelous statements.[99] The United States has generally enjoyed a high degree of social stability, despite periods of considerable upheaval, so Americans can afford more latitude for dangerous speech than can societies where the fabric of human decency is at risk of unraveling. Different perspectives on freedom of the press (and speech) prevail in nations beset with the potential for serious violence or genocide. Take Rwanda in 1994. There is a serious claim that the slaughter among ethnic groups was aided by broadcast media inciting hatred and encouraging violence. The U.S. special assistant for Africa at the time, Donald Steinberg, has said that he wanted to take action, including "jamming the radio station broadcasting tribal hate messages."[100] An interesting legal development was the United Nations' adoption of a resolution in 2006 declaring that all nations have the "responsibility to protect" their own citizens from mass atrocities and providing further that the failure to meet that responsibility would justify the intervention of the international community to establish protection.[101] It might well be that this could justify the international community acting to "censor" media within a country when grave acts of mass violence are threatened.

All of this leads to a larger point, namely, that the more the press from the United States enters the global arena, both to discover the news and to report the news at home and abroad, the more it will encounter policies about and practices of censorship that are fundamentally different from the system of freedom of the press developed in the United States in the twentieth century. Let me state a premise that I will take up in more detail in the next chapter: Americans want and need the nation's press to be engaged journalistically with the wider world. This will enhance Americans' ability both to understand and to act within the increasingly interconnected global society and to help the broader world develop in beneficial ways. But this will not be easy, because from the standpoint of press censorship, much of the world today looks very much like the United States looked in the early years of the twentieth century. In that sense, the twenty-first century can be seen as a recapitulation on a global scale of the American struggle during the last century to embrace a commitment to freedom of press and speech that was "uninhibited, robust, and wide-open." In the twentieth century, as we have seen, Americans had to confront state and federal efforts to prohibit the press from publishing state secrets, from commenting on trials, from publishing falsehoods, from contributing to social strife, and from impugning the government and its officers. The question now is: What happens when Americans' interest in knowing what is occurring in the global arena collides with the rest of the world, which does not accept the U.S. conception of press freedom?

This is not a problem we can avoid. The technology of communication is leading us in this direction. The Internet, especially, is global by its nature, and the more the press moves to this platform, the more this problem will arise. There are already signs of the future in current clashes. Notably and disturbingly, Google, operating principally out of California, with only a few machines around the world, and offering a single platform for the world to access, finds itself under indictment and in litigation in various jurisdictions around the world for violating local censorship laws (including in Italy for invasion of privacy and in Turkey for publishing material insulting "Turkishness").[102]

Another revealing case involves a book published in the United States that resulted in litigation against its author in another country. Rachel Ehrenfeld, an American author, wrote *Funding Evil: How Terrorism Is Financed—And How to Stop It*. Although published only in the United States, the book was listed on Amazon.com, and some two dozen copies were ordered in Britain through that site.[103] British libel law, as I have mentioned, is very permissive toward suits by individuals who claim they have been defamed (such as by placing the burden of proving truth on the author).[104] In her book, Ehrenfeld had accused a Saudi businessman, Khalid bin Mahfouz, of funding terrorism, and he brought a libel action against her in British courts. Ehrenfeld did not appear in court nor at the trial. The British court entered a judgment against her and awarded damages of $225,000. Ehrenfeld brought an action in a U.S. court seeking a declaratory judgment that the British libel judgment would not be enforceable here. The case became entangled in technical procedural questions (about declaratory judgments, jurisdiction, and so on).[105] Legislation was introduced in the New York state legislature that would authorize courts to give declaratory judgments against foreign libel judgments when the speech would be constitutionally protected here. In 2008, the governor of New York, David Paterson, signed a bill called the Libel Terrorism Protection Act.[106] Senators Arlen Specter and Joe Lieberman introduced a similar bill in the U.S. Congress and wrote an op-ed piece in the *Wall Street Journal* arguing that it is not "in our interest to permit the balance struck in America to be upset or circumvented by foreign courts."[107]

Floyd Abrams, the noted First Amendment lawyer who represented Ehrenfeld, also wrote an op-ed piece, explaining why the case was disturbingly representative of a wider trend. He acknowledged that reasonable nations can come to different judgments about the proper balance between reputation and free speech. But he warned that "a serious problem has surfaced" with those differing judgments. "In recent years," he continued, "England has become a choice venue for libel plaintiffs from around the world, including those who seek to intimidate critics whose works would be protected in the U.S. but might not in that country."[108]

These examples illustrate that it is impossible to avoid censorship on a major scale throughout the world. And yet the press—and the American press in particular—is attracting more and more of a global audience, and as this happens, the obstacles to its expansion will become increasingly evident.

This brings me to the subject of the emergence of global media, which can be expected to grow tremendously over the next several decades. The principal international media players in the United States are CNN (which claims a worldwide audience of over 150 million) and news organizations emphasizing financial news (such as the *Wall Street Journal* and Bloomberg News). Both *Newsweek* and *Time* magazines have international editions, each reaching a few million readers.[109] The *New York Times* publishes the *International Herald Tribune*, which has a very limited circulation.[110] Thus, at this point, the private U.S. media have not ventured very far into the global marketplace.

Other countries have been more aggressive in this regard. China's government-sponsored television network, CCTV, is launching major initiatives to become global. The English-language channel of CCTV, CCTV International, in 2009 has approximately 45 million subscribers worldwide, and CCTV also broadcasts in French and Spanish. Recently, CCTV announced the launch of CCTV Arabic International with an audience in twenty-two countries, many of which are very important to China as a source for natural resources and as trade partners.[111]

In the Middle East, the two leading television broadcast networks with a regional and broader distribution are Al Jazeera (with an audience of 40 million Arabic speakers globally),[112] established by the government of Qatar in the 1990s, and Al Arabiya, which was founded and is controlled by Saudi Arabia partly to offset the influence of the perceived anti-Saudi slant of Al Jazeera. Al Jazeera has also developed an English worldwide satellite network, which begins in Malaysia and then moves to Qatar, Britain, and finally the United States, where it is only available by cable in a few markets.[113]

Other examples include News Corporation's Sky television network, which broadcasts around the world in much the same way as CNN, and the British magazine the *Economist*, which has developed a successful niche in the global market (with a circulation of just under 1.4 million).[114]

The largest media group in Spain, Prisa, announced in 2008 that it intends to expand its radio and publishing presence in the United States. It already has radio outlets in Miami and Los Angeles.[115]

The greatest player in building a worldwide press is the BBC and, in particular, its division the BBC World Service. These institutions are uniquely influential on the world stage and in shaping the emerging global press. Established in 1927 through a royal charter, the BBC's stated mission is "[t]o enrich people's lives with programmes and services that inform, educate and entertain."[116] The charter is renewable every ten years. The BBC was the only television station in the United Kingdom until 1955.[117]

The BBC operates under the aegis of the BBC Trust, which was designed to create a "structural separation between oversight of the BBC and delivery of services."[118] There are twelve trustees, who are appointed by the queen on advice from the ministers, following an open appointment process.[119] In order to ensure that the trust remains separate from the management of the BBC, the 2007 royal charter also established an executive board charged with the provision of services. The 2007 charter provides a definition of the "public purposes" to be served by the BBC, including "sustaining citizenship and civil society," "promoting education and learning," "stimulating creativity and cultural excellence," "representing the U.K., its nations, regions and communities," and "bringing the U.K. to the world and the world to the U.K." The independence clause of the royal charter states: "The BBC shall be independent in all matters concerning the content of its output, the times and manner in which this is supplied, and in the management of its affairs."[120] The BBC is primarily funded by license fees paid by all households that own a television set. For 2009, the yearly fee was set at £142.5 per household. This fee yields over £3 billion annually.[121]

Although the BBC distributes some of its programs internationally, the BBC World Service was established specifically to broadcast to a world audience (in the late twentieth century, it was permitted to broadcast within Britain as well). The World Service is not funded by the license fees but by the Foreign and Commonwealth Office through a grant-in-aid, which amounted to approximately £280 million in 2007–2008.[122]

Although the BBC World Service also has journalistic independence, the agreement with Parliament stipulates that the foreign secretary shall have input into the countries and languages in which the World Service will broadcast. The framework agreement also provides that the BBC "must consult and co-operate with the Foreign Secretary and obtain from her such information regarding (a) international developments, (b) conditions in countries outside the U.K., and (c) the policies of Her Majesty's Government in its international relations, as the BBC needs to help it plan and prepare the provision of the World Service in the public interest." Furthermore:

> [The] BBC must agree with the Foreign Secretary, and publish general long-term objectives for the World Service, including— (a) the provision of an accurate, unbiased and independent news service covering international and national developments; (b) the presentation of a balanced British view of those developments; and (c) accurate and effective representation of British life, institutions, and achievements.[123]

The BBC World Service currently broadcasts on radio, television, and online, providing news and information in thirty-two languages and reaching audiences of 40 million in English and 180 million in all languages (roughly one-half of these through shortwave radio and the rest through a variety of other media, such as FM and satellite broadcasts).[124] In 2005, the BBC World Service decided to close ten foreign-language services (Bulgarian, Croatian, Czech, Greek, Hungarian, Kazakh, Polish, Slovak, Slovene, and Thai) in order to free up funds to create new BBC Arabic and Persian (Farsi) television news channels.[125] The BBC World Service's Arabic- and Farsi-language news services are the first international television stations to be publicly funded. They are available to anyone with a satellite dish or cable connection in the respective regions. Both services were launched in 2008. The British Parliament committed an additional £70 million over the period of 2008–2011 to assist with the creation of these new stations.[126] Already by the summer of 2009, and the political crisis in Iran, the BBC Persian channel was "reaching a daily audience of six million to eight million Iranians—a powerful fraction of viewers in Iran, with its population of 70 million."[127]

Both the BBC and the BBC World Service also operate under the general broadcast regulatory authority of the Office of Communications and the Communications Act of 2003, which provides for codes "covering harm, offence, privacy, and fair treatment in programmes" and "quotas to be agreed for each public service broadcaster, concerning levels of news and current affairs programmes and programmes for audiences in different parts of the UK, levels of original productions and productions outside the M25 [greater London]."[128] I have heard many people from around the world say that they grew up listening to the BBC World News, usually in the static-filled atmosphere of shortwave radio, as their only source of objective information. The BBC World Service is known for its very strong commitment to editorial independence from the British government.

Today, the BBC World Service is a significant source of international news even in the United States. Over 250 public radio stations carry programming from the BBC, the BBC World Service, and Britain's Independent Television Network (ITN), in particular for their coverage of global news. Since 1996, U.S. public radio stations, with a weekly audience of about 16 million, have broadcast an afternoon program called *The World*, which is created by the BBC

World Service in collaboration with WGBH in Boston and Public Radio International (which was founded in 1983 by four state public networks).[129] In other words, for many in the United States, news about the world comes courtesy of the British media and hence British citizens. This also highlights the fact that the more Americans rely on foreign press for international news the more we will be affected by the different—and more limited—free press traditions around the world.

This leads us to the less visible side of U.S. engagement with the world: the various U.S. government–sponsored international broadcast channels, which are overseen by the Broadcasting Board of Governors (BBG). (The BBG is composed of four Democratic appointees, four Republican appointees, and the secretary of state. It is "the independent federal agency responsible for all U.S. government and government sponsored, non-military, international broadcasting.") These broadcasting programs, which collectively received $671 million in government funds in 2008, are part of a long tradition of U.S. government-created and -funded propaganda media, which began with the Voice of America in 1942 and Radio Free Europe, which first broadcast in 1950. Other channels now include Radio Sawa (Middle East), Radio Free Asia, Radio Marti/TV Marti (Cuba), and the Al Hurra satellite television channel, which was created in 2004 for the Middle East.[130]

These broadcast channels have walked an uneasy line between propagandistic purposes and attempts to provide objective reporting and information to regions of the world that lack an independent media. Radio Free Europe has always had a more propagandistic bent than the other channels, whereas Voice of America has aimed to provide objective content, while serving the diplomatic interests of the United States. In 2009 Voice of America broadcasts in forty-five languages to an estimated audience of 134 million.[131] The VOA charter was created in 1960 and signed into law in 1976. It reads in part:

The long-range interests of the United States are served by communicating directly with the peoples of the world by radio. To be effective, the Voice of America must win the attention and respect of listeners. These principles will therefore govern Voice of America (VOA) broadcasts:

(1) VOA will serve as a consistently reliable and authoritative source of news. VOA news will be accurate, objective and comprehensive.

(2) VOA will represent America, not any single segment of American society, and will therefore present a balanced and comprehensive projection of significant American thought and institutions.

(3) VOA will present the policies of the United States clearly and effectively, and will also present responsible discussions and opinion on these policies.[132]

Radio Free Europe, on the other hand, was initially directed by the Central Intelligence Agency and the State Department, with the explicit function of reaching countries in Europe under communist control during the Cold War in the 1950s. It currently broadcasts in twenty-eight languages to twenty countries, including Iran, Iraq, Afghanistan, Russia, and the Central Asian republics. Its formally stated mission is "to promote democratic values and institutions by disseminating factual information and ideas." It aims to provide "objective news, analysis, and discussion of domestic and regional issues crucial to successful democratic and free-market transformations," to strengthen "civil societies by projecting democratic values," to combat "ethnic and religious intolerance and promote mutual understanding among peoples," to provide "a model for local media," and to foster "closer ties between the countries of the region and the world's established democracies."[133]

The inherent tension in the missions of these government media has been particularly explosive in the case of Al Hurra, a satellite television channel headquartered in Springfield, Virginia, and aimed at twenty-two Arab countries, from Morocco to the Persian Gulf, with a total population of 170 million. Created in 2004, Al Hurra was designed, according to a State Department official, to "bring to the Arab-speaking world…a free press, to show them what a free press is like, to report in many cases stories that are not being reported by their own press or by the pan-Arab press, much of which is quite inflammatory, and to explain American policy and what's going on in America in general."[134] While meant to compete with Al Jazeera and Al Arabiya and despite a yearly budget of about $100 million, it has attracted only about 2 percent of its target audience (excluding Iraq).[135] In its short life, Al Hurra has faced a host of criticisms of its subject matter, lack of expertise, weak journalistic credibility, and large operating expenses. In 2008, CBS's *60 Minutes* joined with the newly established nonprofit investigative organization ProPublica in a report on now wasteful and ineffective Al Hurra was with Arab viewers and to "blow the whistle on the latest American misadventure on the international airwaves."[136] The *Washington Post* published its own similar investigation that week that found that "after spending nearly $500 million, the channel has been mismanaged, has broadcast unchecked anti-Israel rhetoric, and is not competing effectively in an ever-growing Arab media market." The report found that the low audience numbers could be attributed to the perception in the Middle East that Al Hurra is the U.S. government channel, as opposed to an alternative, independent media outlet.[137]

One of the important features of this system is that these government-funded broadcasters are restricted by the Smith-Mundt Act from the domestic dissemination of their programs and can provide archived copies of content to the public only twelve years after broadcast.[138] In 1994, the International Broadcasting Act reorganized all nonmilitary, government-funded, international broadcasting to come under the purview of the U.S. Information Agency, while creating the Broadcasting Board of Governors to oversee the broadcasting. In 2000, the USIA was folded into the State Department, while the BBG became a stand-alone agency.[139]

One of the debates surrounding Al Hurra is whether there has been too little domestic accountability for its programming and operations. As reported by *60 Minutes*, although the State Department provides guidelines on coverage, they are difficult to enforce because the channel is not seen in the United States and no translation is provided to government overseers or Congress. The State Department has a team watching Al Hurra, but there are no fluent Arabic speakers on it nor in the BBG.[140] In 2008 a bill was proposed in Congress that would have amended the International Broadcasting Act of 1994 and specifically exempt the Middle East Broadcasting Network (which produces Al Hurra) and the Voice of America Persian Service from the ban on domestic dissemination.[141] But greater domestic oversight to ensure that the content is more in line with U.S. interests will not address the journalistic credibility problem that plagues Al Hurra and may simply reinforce the perception that Al Hurra is the mouthpiece of the U.S. government.

In sum, we are facing the emergence of a global society, with the technological capacity to provide a free and independent press to a world in desperate need of such an institution, but there is also a myriad of laws, policies, practices, and conditions that inhibit and impede that from happening. Without a central, overriding system of constitutional protections, there is a risk of a collapse to the bottom, where jurisdictions that have the least degree of freedom will undermine the freedom of those that value it the most. Over the course of the twentieth century, it was precisely this kind of phenomenon that led the Supreme Court and Congress to create a national system in which the press could develop and thrive out of the stifling multitude of separate state and municipal approaches.

This situation poses a significant challenge to the United States and the world. For a society uniquely committed to unconstrained public debate and for which knowledge of the entire world is increasingly vital, we must now see how we can achieve this goal—to make it a shared principle as well as a working reality—in a world that is not in full agreement with the American conception of a free press. How can we make the principle a reality regardless of frontiers?

CHAPTER FOUR

The Touchstone

FREEDOM OF THE PRESS is entering a new stage in its development. As we have seen, the idea was forged out of a series of judicial
decisions and societal forces over the course of the last century. The
Supreme Court created a jurisprudence rooted in a rationale emphasizing the benefits to society of a certain kind of national public
forum (captured in the phrase "uninhibited, robust, and wide-
open"), in which the press would play a major role. The press could
count on the courts to protect it against the myriad of efforts to
censor it, whether these efforts were to preserve domestic peace and
security, to protect individual reputations, to insulate government
processes from public scrutiny, to preserve the fairness of judicial
proceedings, or to further any number of other interests. But the
press was also left, more or less, to its own inventiveness in gathering
information. And, in the limited realm of the broadcast media, where
both privately and publicly funded models existed, the federal
government was permitted to regulate the press, in the public
interest, to enhance the marketplace of ideas, but not otherwise to

play the role of censor (with the significant exception of indecency regulations).

Within the contours of this constitutional and public policy regime, other forces helped to shape the American press. The press embraced the ideal of serving a public purpose and having a quasi-official role. Moreover, it began to function as a fourth branch of government and clung to its independence from government oversight. As we have seen, economic forces produced concerns about the excessive concentration of power in the media. But along with the trajectory of monopolization came the development of journalistic values that embraced concepts of fairness, balance, and objectivity in the reporting of news, as well as the financial strength to build specialized expertise and to provide deeper coverage of national and international issues.

With the advent of the Internet and the rise of globalization, the environment in which the press operated in the twentieth century has been changing in fundamental ways. The need for more comprehensive coverage of the emerging world community is greater than ever, and the capacity of new communications technologies to reach wider audiences at lower cost has expanded dramatically. At the same time, however, the financial structure that worked so well in the twentieth century is being undermined. As a result, the press has displayed an alarming incapacity to fulfill its public trust of keeping Americans informed about the state of the world. The need for a vigorous, all-present, independent press is greater than ever, yet the capacity of the press to meet that need has been put in serious question. Moreover, as we move toward a world in which the United States is increasingly integrated in and dependent on the actions of other nations, we are re-encountering a realm of censorship that is reminiscent of the world as it existed in the United States at the beginning of the twentieth century. How should we conceive of and implement the principle of freedom of the press in the twenty-first century? That is the subject of this chapter.

I

We need to start with some clarity about our premises. There are seven critical premises. The first is that we need a free and independent press. Certainly, as long as there is democracy or government based on some even minimal level of consent of the people, the press is a necessity. Someone must provide us with factual information and analysis of what is happening in the world while upholding values of—in the language of the Pulitzer Prize—"honesty, accuracy, and fairness."[1] The objective gathering and reporting of news—a relatively recent historical development—is by far the most vulnerable function of journalism in today's realities. In addition, we need a free press to provide a common forum for thought and discussion. A free press affords an opportunity that is essential to a democracy: It helps to create a robust public forum in which we test our capacity for tolerance by confronting viewpoints and speech behavior with which we disagree and find objectionable. As I argued earlier, that is one of the ways in which we develop the qualities of mind that are essential to democracy, to social interactions that transcend the arena of speech, and to combating the natural inclinations that lead to an authoritarian mindset.

The second and third premises are related: For the press to flourish, it must be an *institution*, and it must have a *culture of journalism as a profession*. These premises go hand in hand. The concept of an institution can encompass many different forms, but it starts with the importance of having organizations large and powerful enough to be able effectively to monitor and check the authority of the state. For this reason, the press cannot be composed of a multitude of isolated individuals or small organizations, however much each may be committed to high-quality journalism. At least some of the organizations that make up the press must have sufficient scale to have serious newsgathering ability and to bring together multiple centers of expertise, knowledge, and capacity. The simple fact is that there are some things we want that only big organizations can provide (which is not at all to deny the benefits of a multiplicity of voices as well). All of this is important also for the development of a professional culture of journalism, which is fundamentally a collective and individual commitment to provide the public with objective and independent reporting and analysis. The larger whole reinforces the values for each individual member of the professional community.

These three premises—(1) our need for a press, (2) including institutions with a certain scale and (3) a dedication to a professional culture of journalism—may seem self-evident, but it is important to emphasize them because there is at times a too casual and erroneous assumption that it would be just fine if the press as we have known it were to disappear and be replaced by thousands or even millions of individual Web sites from which we could each tailor our own specific "press." It is a serious mistake to assume that a multitude of individual or small-scale Web sites would serve the same purpose as the traditional press, just as it would be a mistake to think that universities could be replaced by many individual Web sites, each offering specialized knowledge in an atomized manner. The way in which knowledge is organized, developed, and conveyed in the context of a large and complex institution devoted to journalistic or scholarly values is radically different from the way knowledge would be transmitted and understood in a highly dispersed system. Myriad Web sites can enhance public debate, but they cannot replace the role of the institutional press.

The fourth premise restates a point made earlier: We cannot expect the free market alone to sustain the press as we have come to define it. Insofar as we want the press to fulfill a public purpose, the marketplace by itself will not make that happen. Broadcasting, as we have seen, has never been left completely to the market, and newspapers have acquired a quasi-public role precisely because they achieved a kind of natural monopoly status. It is, of course, a matter of strong debate whether public support and/or regulation are preferable to reliance on the forces of the marketplace, and that issue is properly debatable with respect to the press. I will have more to say about this in a moment. The point I want to make now is that we cannot expect to see a press like the one we have produced by leaving it entirely to the market.

A fifth premise is that we do not know how the forces now at work, if left alone, will reshape the press in the future. There is no doubt that we are experiencing a transformative period in the history of the press. But it remains to be played out in the real world: Finances may stabilize, Web revenues may grow sufficiently to sustain major news organizations, the press may reconfigure itself through mergers and bankruptcies, universities may assume responsibility to become "teaching news organizations" in the way medical schools run teaching hospitals, people of enormous wealth may take the press on as philanthropic activities—or we may be headed toward a steady process of decay and the death of the traditional press. Google (and others) may do to the news what Amazon did to books and iTunes did to music.

At the moment, the financially strongest publications appear to be those with a primary focus on economic and business news. It is a heartening sign for the viability of the press generally that the leaders among this group are expanding their coverage of political news, out of a correct perception that you cannot understand economics (a driving force of globalization) without understanding politics. Yet, because the reverse is also true, and because the angle of vision almost always depends upon where one starts, it would be a pity if the marketplace of journalism did not sustain a politics-based perspective as well. We do not know the future, but the situation is clearly of the utmost urgency and calls for our full attention and efforts to shape events to the extent we can in order to preserve the great tradition of a free press, which, once lost, would be exceedingly difficult (and maybe impossible) to recreate.

A sixth and key premise is that, just as a fundamental project of the twentieth century was to create a *national* system of a free press in the United States, a central challenge of the twenty-first century will be to create a *global* system of a free press for the emerging global society. We need to think in terms of a global public forum that is uninhibited, robust, and wide-open and a press that serves that forum. Such a goal has many elements. As a practical matter, and even as a First Amendment matter, it means bringing more news about the world to U.S. citizens. That can happen most directly by the American press increasing its coverage of global issues. And the best way for this to occur is for the American press to have a sustained and permanent newsgathering presence in all regions of the world and the specialized knowledge and expertise to interpret the news it gathers.

For Americans to become better informed about the world, however, there must be a vigorous foreign press, and Americans must hear more of what it has to report. The United States condemns the censorship of foreign media as a violation of human rights. That is laudable, but it is a perspective that puts a distance between us and them that is anachronistic. Americans need to change the way we think in this regard. When the rights of foreign media are curtailed, *our* rights are threatened. That's what globalization means. Much of what Americans will know and need to know about the world will come only from a free and independent press throughout the world. Often the foreign media will be the source of reporting that will alert the U.S. media to what is journalistically important. Americans must, therefore, see the foreign press as our press, as important to the United States as it is to the society in which it resides.

In an increasingly interconnected, global society, therefore, censorship anywhere can become censorship everywhere. This is precisely what the Court saw in *New York Times v. Sullivan*. As the United States moved toward a national public forum, libel law in Alabama could chill expression in New York and elsewhere. Now, it is Turkey or Thailand that can do the same in the global public forum. We need, accordingly, to understand the globally inhibiting effects of censorship in any part of the world and to try to do for this new forum what *Sullivan* did to facilitate the shift to a national forum in the United States.

The seventh premise is that freedom of information is the "touchstone," to use the language of the United Nations, for much of what we strive for in the world: It is the key to securing other rights and to serving other ends.[2] We are threatened by authoritarian and corrupt governments, in part because they create instability and disenchantment. We are concerned about poverty and disease, in part because they are tragic and breed instability and terrorism. We seek free trade among nations, in part because it advances human well-being and provides incentives against natural impulses towards isolationism and conflict. We want openness and transparency, in part because information is crucial to the ability to solve problems and to make wise decisions. We need to promote the spread of knowledge and information, because in general people *behave better* when they *know more*. To achieve these and so many other goals and ends of life a free press is actually a necessary condition. Consider just one.

In a 2007 book entitled *The Bottom Billion*, Paul Collier addresses the question of what can be done to improve the condition of the billion or so people on the planet (mostly living in sub-Saharan Africa) who "are living and dying in fourteenth-century conditions." He notes the benefits and limits of direct foreign aid and humanitarian assistance,[3] the problem of economic decline induced by too much reliance on a single valuable resource (such as oil or gold),[4] and the long-lingering devastating consequences of civil wars.[5] His principal concern, however, is with maintaining checks against the typically bad and corrupt governments in the states where the bottom billion live. Essential to the creation of a stable, self-governing society is a free press:

> In the societies of the bottom billion the key media are probably the radio channels and increasingly television. One rare and dramatic story from Peru illustrates this. The government of Alberto Fujimori was notably corrupt.... The Fujimori government set out to systematically undermine each check and balance that restrained it. It bribed members of parliament, judges, newspaper editors, and the staff of radio stations and television stations. If there was a restraint, the government undermined it. The amount it was prepared to pay reflected its view of the importance of each restraint.... Where the Fujimori regime put most of its money is probably where we should be most vigilant.... Where the zeros rolled out on the checks was to buy the television stations. There were ten stations, and the government bought them at nearly a million dollars each per month.... So for the government it was the television news that was the vital restraint to control. Was this paranoia? No, it turned out that the government was quite right. We know because the government had only bothered to buy the nine biggest television channels—it decided not to bother with the tenth, a tiny financial satellite service with only ten thousand subscribers. That is how the government fell. Someone leaked a video of [a government official] bribing a judge, and it was broadcast on this one television channel. Protest escalated uncontrollably. So in Peru the key restraint upon the government was the media, and among the media, it was television.[6]

This is a story that can be told again and again—how an independent press helped to topple an authoritarian regime by providing information to citizens.

The connection between a free press and stable democracies is borne out in the scholarship on the subject. One important study has established not only a correlation between press freedom and lack of war (both civil and interstate) but also that levels of press freedom are predictive of democratization.[7] Thus, the critical link between a free press and our need to prevent the worst of human tragedies (such as civil wars and genocide) and to make the most of human relationships (such as free trade) is borne out by experience, serious reflection and scholarship.[8] The upshot is that *everyone*, no matter what their goal, should be enlisted as an advocate of freedom of the press.

II

With these premises in hand, let us turn to the task of providing a framework for how to think about the press and about freedom of the press in the twenty-first century. As we have seen, developing this framework has several dimensions to it. We must decide how much to carry forward, change, or add to the constitutional law and public policy we have inherited. We must do that while also taking into account the changed circumstances in which we now find the press, a context that seems certain to shift even more in the coming years. Most important, our thinking must encompass the fundamental fact that the goal must now include not only preserving and enhancing a free press in the United States, with expanding coverage of the emerging global society, but also the fulfillment of such a press on a global scale. All of this will take time to unfold. It is a critical project for the twenty-first century.

A

We start with the role that the U.S. Supreme Court (and, by exten-
sion, courts in general) can and should play in developing a free
press in the twenty-first century. We have reviewed what the Court
did in the twentieth century—how it helped to create the conditions for a national public forum, one characterized by extraordinary
protections and openness, with opportunities for speakers to
confront us with speech we may dislike and even deservedly
condemn. The Court then infused this forum with fundamental
meaning. It stressed fulfilling the commitment to self-government,
improving the odds of finding truth, and acquiring, in the hurly-
burly of this uniquely unregulated zone of behavior, moderation of
our natural authoritarian tendencies, which if unchecked can undermine and even destroy a pluralistic community. In following this
overall course, the Court deployed a number of strategies: It used
small issues as opportunities to address big ideas; while taking major
steps, it left itself room to change course if circumstances and
further reflection merited it; and it was experimental, unwilling to
be a slave to the pure logic of its principles, cautiously supportive of
laws intended to enhance the national forum, and eager to embrace
the inevitably messy world of checks and balances over a single,
uniform system.

Now, the Court must build on these precedents and strategies in
a new era presenting fresh challenges. It is difficult at this early stage
to know precisely what will be needed to sustain a free and independent press. I have the sense, as I will explain in a moment, that
public funding will be a central part of any strategy. For this, the
Court will need to build on its decisions insulating the recipients of
public funding from improper controls over content.

But the most important item on the Court's agenda is to begin
the process of making the shift from the constitutional paradigm of

a national public forum to a global one. We need the Court to intro-
duce us to this new reality; we need a *New York Times v. Sullivan* for
the twenty-first century. As I have said, we are now in a world in
which censorship in China is as threatening to First Amendment
interests as censorship in Alabama or Nebraska was found to be
some decades ago. Of course, the Court's power to deal with this
new reality is diminished. But it is far from nonexistent. I will have
several suggestions to make in the discussion ahead, but here are
some opening observations.

Once the Court defines a constitutional need for an open global
forum, this will unleash the creativity of the legal system to bring
appropriate cases to the fore. Opportunities to shape the system will
emerge, and the Court can at times, as it has in the past, speak to
the government's affirmative responsibility to advance this goal.
Already, we can see the possibilities. A Court sensitive to this
perspective would, for example, give less weight to the traditional
principle of comity in enforcing foreign legal judgments and refuse
enforcement in cases where a similar case in the United States
would result in protection for speech under the First Amendment.
This is, for example, the standard recognized in legislation that has
been adopted in New York and Illinois involving British libel judgments brought to U.S. courts for enforcement.[9]

Taking a broader perspective on what the Court can do, I would
emphasize two points. First, the Court must appreciate the power of
the example that the First Amendment sets for the world. The
essence of this power, I believe, is in the very idea of a press that is
objective and independent—a press that is critical of government
authority and that provides access to ordinary citizens and to a
multiplicity of views. A 2006 decision by the British House of Lords
on libel, providing significantly more protections for the press when
discussing public figures, is a good illustration of the potential grav-
itational pull of American law.

Second, the Court must speak more directly to the broader world. We need actively and deliberately to try to influence the rest of the world to embrace what we have come to believe is vital to a good society. A good way to start is for the Court to acknowledge that Americans have gone through the same process we are urging on others. The United States developed its modern commitment to freedom of press and speech over many years. American progress over time can serve as a model, and as a shortcut, for other nations that are struggling toward a more mature understanding of freedom of expression.

The Court should also rethink how it articulates the basic rationales for its choices under the First Amendment. There is no need for insistence on a single theory. The First Amendment, and the principle of freedom of the press specifically, reflects a number of different values and societal objectives, some of which may be more appealing on a global scale than others. We cannot expect all of the world to embrace a system of Madisonian self-government, with sovereignty understood to reside in the people. It would be futile and counterproductive to link the concept of a free press solely to that commitment as we search for a common global norm. The fact is that an independent and free press can exist comfortably in many forms of government, and it would be unfortunate if people and societies around the world concluded that the U.S. conception of freedom of the press is irrelevant to them because *Sullivan*'s rationale is inapplicable to their political systems. An emphasis on how a system of openness helps to moderate authoritarian tendencies and helps to generate capacities to deal with social conflict may meet with a better reception in many societies.

Beyond this, the Court might also draw on the language and concepts in current international conventions and laws, which I will discuss in more detail later. Most of these documents proclaim, in the words of the Universal Declaration of Human Rights (UDHR), that "everyone has the right to freedom of opinion and expression," including "freedom...to seek, receive and impart information and ideas through any media and regardless of frontiers."[10] This is not linked to any particular theory of democratic self-government; it is simply a right of individual citizens throughout the world. The Supreme Court should explicitly acknowledge this way of conceiving of freedom of the press.

From an internal standpoint, the Court should adhere to its general approach to building freedom of the press. As a society, the United States has thrived with the decisions establishing the first pillar. Overall, the Court should stay the course.

Of course, there will be significant issues in further refining the first pillar. We can expect that concerns about the new communication technologies will be raised. Already, with the increasing centrality of the Internet in our system of expression, we are hearing reasonable concerns about whether the fragmentation of social discourse (the decline of a few commonly read or viewed media outlets) will deprive us as a society of shared information and experiences, leaving us less able to discuss issues, less exposed to diverse viewpoints, and more inclined to connect primarily, or only, with those with whom we agree. This might increase our conviction that we are right and others wrong and therefore might breed intolerance. Some also express concern over the way in which communication on the Internet seems to encourage venomous attitudes and to facilitate criminal and terrorist acts. These are serious concerns. We must recognize, however, that every time a new communication technology emerges, so do alarms about its potentially destructive impact and calls to revise our notion of freedom. Usually, these fears turn out to be exaggerated or are dealt with successfully in other ways. Overall, the balance we have struck should only be strengthened through future cases.

B

The second pillar is different. The time has come—especially in light of U.S. needs in the global public forum—to change First Amendment doctrine to recognize an affirmative right of the press to have access to information under the control of the government and to otherwise engage in newsgathering. As we saw in chapter 1, while the Court held that newsgathering is protected to some extent, a narrow majority of the Court insisted that such protection is minimal.

The principal arguments supporting the current doctrine are as follows. First, the Free Press Clause confers no special rights on the press beyond those generally afforded citizens under the Free Speech Clause. Second, it would be difficult, maybe even impossible, and possibly even dangerous to the values underlying the First Amendment to define as a constitutional matter who is and is not the "press." Third, it would be extremely difficult for courts to review the myriad instances in which the press might claim that newsworthy information was being withheld unreasonably by the government. Finally, courts should mandate press access only in those rare circumstances, such as criminal trials, in which the proceeding or information has historically been open to the public and the press. To this moment, these arguments have carried the day. And some of these points arguably carry even more weight in today's circumstances. How, for example, can we separate the "press" among the proliferating Web sites that now claim that they, too, are in the business of "reporting news" to the public?

On balance, however, the arguments on the other side have become even more compelling. It is important to begin with how things work in the everyday world. As a practical matter, statutory rights of access for the public and the press are now common. Freedom of information acts abound across federal and state governments. More to the point, reporters are regularly accorded special access to newsworthy events, such as presidential press conferences, and are even "embedded" in military campaigns, as they were at the start of the Iraq war. All of this works reasonably well, despite the dire predictions of definitional dilemmas, vexing conflicts, and slippery-slope consequences. To be sure, many issues must be resolved in making this system work. But the transparency achieved is, on balance, indisputably beneficial.

There are, moreover, good reasons arising out of recent U.S. history that make it imperative to begin the twenty-first century with a broader recognition of a constitutional right of press access to information. There is now ample evidence that the Bush administration developed policies and practices to maintain secrecy about fundamentally important government actions, including some that posed grave threats to constitutional liberties. The administration's efforts in the early parts of the war in Afghanistan to exclude the press and the military's unreviewable decisions to limit, arrest, and detain members of the press during the war in Iraq are significant instances of secrecy at the expense of public knowledge. It is of the highest importance in a democracy that there be a constitutional right of the press to have reasonable access to the most consequential actions undertaken by the government (going to war most certainly falls in that category), such that the government cannot act in secret with total impunity and that there is a judicial forum in which the balance of interests in these situations can be adjudicated. Equally important, denying the press meaningful access to critical war zones, such as Afghanistan and Iraq, undermines the perception abroad of the U.S. commitment to a free and independent press, making America look the same as authoritarian regimes—that is, whenever the government does something really important, such as go to war or invade a country, the United States too denies the press access or allows it only on terms that will maximize the positive spin the government seeks.

It is not enough merely to urge the government voluntarily to give the press access to newsworthy events and information. The government's policy of voluntarily embedding journalists at the beginning of the Iraq war teaches two important lessons. First, it undermines the government's argument in other circumstances that the presence of the press cannot be accommodated. The reality is that this is largely a matter of whether the government wants to accommodate the press. The issue, therefore, is whether the government should be able to exclude the press when it suits its interests, free of any constitutional responsibilities. Second, there is a significant difference between the press being present as a matter of right and being present at the whim of the unchecked authority of the government. The substance of what is reported will be influenced by the terms under which the reporting takes place. It is a natural human tendency to curry favor with those who have power. It would, in other words, better ensure the independence and objectivity of the press to make its role a matter of constitutional right than of governmental grace.

Another facet of this aspect of freedom of the press deserves attention. I noted in the earlier discussion of the Court's rejection of a right of access that it created a seemingly awkward system in which the press can publish whatever it learns, but the government can withhold from the press (and the public) whatever it wishes. Apart from how this system disrupts the flow of information to the public, and apart from the ways in which this encourages government secrecy, it also creates an unseemly incentive for the press to encourage government employees to unlawfully leak secret government information. The Court could have held that government employees have a First Amendment right to disclose newsworthy information, including classified documents, to the press. But the Court rejected this position (and, even if it hadn't, the opposite approach would still have resulted in a situation in which the press would have to find a willing employee in order to gain access).

Under the current state of the law, the press has an incentive to encourage leaks so that it and the public can reap the benefits of publication, while the leaker is left to face possible prosecution and punishment. Although few leakers are ever caught or prosecuted, the press is put in a position where its incentives are to undermine the rule of law. The most famous articulation of the post–*Pentagon Papers* system—Alexander Bickel's statement that "if we ordered [disclosure of government information] we would have to sacrifice one of two contending values—privacy or public discourse—which are ultimately irreconcilable"—is not an argument but a blunt description of reality.[11] Of course, there are competing interests (government secrecy versus public knowledge), but this is true whenever the government seeks to limit the freedoms of speech and press. Nothing in this particular conflict necessitates resolving it by imposing this disorderly cat-and-mouse system between the press and the government. A better system would be for the Supreme Court to initiate a constitutional process in which these competing values could be weighed against each other and resolved in a judicially sanctioned manner. An orderly system, in short, is preferable.

It is a reasonable concern that a right to newsgathering could lead to so many press demands that the courts would be overwhelmed with cases and the government overly burdened with defending legitimate interests in secrecy. But we cannot know what would happen under such a system until it is tried. A lot will depend, of course, on how the right is defined. We can take comfort, however, from the fact that we have successfully managed exactly this state of affairs under the freedom of information acts that have existed now for several decades.

This brings me to the question of how the Court should develop this right of access. The Court has often recognized a First Amendment right in situations that seem to open up endless problems of definition. The Public Forum Doctrine is a good analogy. The

Public Forum Doctrine exemplifies how the Court has developed an affirmative duty under the First Amendment requiring the government to help expand the opportunities for speech. This doctrine compels the government to allow speech to take place on some public property, such as streets, parks, and sidewalks.[12] The Public Forum Doctrine is a precedent for protections on the newsgathering side of freedom of the press.

The Public Forum Doctrine is also helpful because of how the Court has gone about delineating the boundaries of the doctrine. The Court first announced the doctrine in a case involving the question of whether the public has a right of access to speak in public streets and parks, even though that use might conflict with a variety of public purposes (free flow of traffic, peace and quiet, control over litter, and so on).[13] The recognition of this right of access carried the potential for the public to claim the right to use all kinds of government property for speech purposes, including public printing presses, speaking in public buses, and speaking in the legislature. Predictably, a number of suits were brought seeking access to a wide variety of public places. But the Court turned away these claims, concluding that the right applies only to places that have been opened up to public speech or have historically been made available for public speech (such as streets and parks).[14] The key point is not that the Court has necessarily drawn the right line in the Public Forum Doctrine, but that it was able to limit the reach of the right in a principled manner that reasonably balances speech and competing interests.

Something similar can be done with a Doctrine of Access to Newsworthy Events and Information. As we have seen, the Court has already recognized a right of the general public and the press to be present at criminal trials,[15] and it has further acknowledged that the press has at least some constitutional protections in the news-gathering process.[16] When a new case comes along involving the public interest in knowing about information under the government's control, the

Court should take the next step and announce a general right of access. A good example that could have been used this way was the dispute between the government and the press over access to the war zone in Afghanistan. Another example was the request by the press to visit military prisons in Iraq.[17] Yet another would have been a press demand to develop a process to adjudicate the military's imprisonment of the AP photojournalist, or to require the government to have reasonable procedures to be followed when members of the press are arrested.

It would be possible for the Court to articulate an important expansion of the freedom of the press in ways that would be responsive to the new realities of the twenty-first century. The current fragility of the financial position of the press ought to be a matter of serious First Amendment concern. According the press special rights of newsgathering could contribute both to maintaining the institution of the press and to providing it with distinctive information in the media marketplace.

And it would represent a momentous shift in focus for the Court to develop a broader newsgathering right in the context of international or global government actions. The Court could speak of the importance of increasing the flow of information about global issues and of widening the American perspective on freedom of the press in a new global society. It would also serve as a powerful example to the world of the degree of commitment in the United States to bringing as much information and knowledge to the public as possible. It is true that, traditionally, the Court has deferred more to the government when the government's interest in limiting speech involves matters of foreign policies, primarily on the reasoning that the courts are less able to evaluate the merits of the asserted interests. But this notion of a line between domestic and foreign interests is precisely what is being erased by globalization. Not only is it increasingly an artificial distinction, but it is counterproductive to the needs of U.S. citizens to participate effectively in decisions in a more integrated world.

C

Turning now to the third pillar, the system of public interest regulation of broadcasting is alive but not entirely well. There is now a strong need to reinvigorate the principles that have governed this domain for over eighty years. The Supreme Court has not signaled any interest in backing away from either *Red Lion* or *Miami Herald*, but the FCC's regulatory system has changed over time. It has been extended in some areas (such as the regulation of "indecency") and retracted in others (most notably with the repeal of the Fairness Doctrine). This has been the result of nearly two decades of socially conservative, free market–oriented appointees, who have generally favored policies of selective regulation with an emphasis on prohibiting certain content based on moral judgments and disfavoring regulations that expand the range of viewpoints and are thought to impinge upon the business interests of broadcast owners. These changes must be reversed.

It is time, first of all, to end the regulation of "indecent" language and images in broadcast programming. The Court should declare this unconstitutional. Because this regulation constitutes censorship of speech beyond what has been constitutionally permitted elsewhere in society, including in public spaces, it is an anomaly. Recall that, in *Cohen v. California*, the Court emphatically rejected California's claim that it could constitutionally prohibit offensive speech in public settings (in *Cohen*, a young person in the halls outside a public courtroom wore a jacket bearing the words "Fuck the Draft" across the back).[18] This was a landmark First Amendment case that has governed since it was decided in 1971.

In *FCC v. Pacifica Foundation*, however, the Court upheld the FCC's power to enforce indecency standards in broadcasting (a position narrowly reaffirmed by the Court in a 2009 decision upholding an FCC regulation that punishes broadcasters for "fleeting expletives" before 10 P.M.).[19] *Pacifica* rests on the flawed idea that indecent language and images on television and radio are more offensive, more intrusive into our lives, and more likely to injure children than the same speech in every other context of our lives.[20] The majority in *Pacifica* mistakenly assumed that the offending speech coming into "the home" (or the car, as was the case in *Pacifica*) is too difficult to avoid through one's own preventive actions. But the ability to change the channel is no different from the ability to turn the page or to avert one's eyes. As *Cohen* held, such self-help remedies are sufficient to safeguard our sensibilities in a robust First Amendment world.[21] *Pacifica* was wrong when it was decided.

Beyond that though, three new facts are now apparent that should lead the Court to jettison this anomaly in the U.S. system. First, the advent of cable and the Internet has created a world filled with experiments in indecent language and images, making broadcast channels seem prudish and quaint by comparison. Second, filters and blocking devices now allow the individual to decide what does and does not enter the home, vastly reducing the justification for government regulation. And, third, the surge in indecency enforcement by the Bush administration's FCC has led to serious self-censorship by broadcasters who are afraid to offend the commission. The Court should end this venture in morals regulation in broadcasting. It is inconsistent with the First Amendment's general commitment to a system of extraordinary protections against censorship and, as such, tends to undermine the overall "public interest" regulatory scheme for broadcasting, which is otherwise admirably focused on *expanding* the range of speech available. (I should note that I am not challenging the regulation of obscenity nor child pornography, insofar as they are regulated in *all* media.)

At the same time, it is important to bring more vigor back into the "public interest" standard and regulations designed to expand the range of voices in these media. There are still regulations governing access and "equal time" for candidates for political office and requiring broadcasters to provide certain programming, such as local news. On the other hand, the FCC has abandoned the Fairness Doctrine, which was designed to ensure that broadcasting would be a forum for comprehensive public debate about "controversial issues of public importance." This must be reversed. Beyond that, we need a renewed national debate about how to help make broadcasting more of a medium for meaningful public discussion. I have always been attracted to the idea that broadcasters should be required to sell time to those wishing to express their views about public issues.

The problem with the broadcast media is, and has always been, its tendency to focus on entertainment rather than public issues. (Radio has a somewhat different trajectory, with a tendency in some stations to adopt ideologically narrow biases.) This is due almost entirely to commercial motives. For the same profit, it is preferable to sell time for detergent ads rather than paid messages about controversial ideas (as the *New Yrok Times* had done with the civil rights advocates who had placed the print advertisement in the *Sullivan* case). The trend among broadcasters not to sell time for political commentary is driven by their fear of offending audiences. Yet the opportunity for the public to express their viewpoints and to hear other viewpoints, directly and in their own voices, is essential to a society committed to the principle of vigorous and engaged public debate. Moreover, as things stand now, discussions are naturally skewed toward the corporate view of the world, as broadcasters readily sell time to companies seeking not only to sell their products but to present positive impressions of their brands and activities. A requirement to sell time equally to those wishing to speak to public issues would help to remedy that imbalance. In order to deal with the inability of citizens to afford the purchase of airtime, a number of solutions are possible, including requiring broadcasters to provide a certain amount of time free or making public funds available.

What is most important is that this facet of our system of broadcast regulation must be taken seriously again. From the Supreme Court, we need a clarification of the rationales of *Red Lion* and *Miami Herald*. The Court must acknowledge the inadequacy of the scarcity rationale and the notion that broadcast regulation is legitimate because the airwaves are a "public resource." For the reasons I gave in chapter 2, these arguments do not withstand serious scrutiny. The Court must say, directly, that under the First Amendment it is not necessary that all communication technologies be structured identically, that there are merits to having multiple approaches to a vigorous press, and that having multiple approaches yields benefits of experimentation, the mutual reinforcement of positive journalistic norms, and checks on the risks of any uniform system.

If we integrate the realities of globalization and the need for more press engagement into the policies of broadcast regulation, several ideas deserve to be considered. Some involve public funding of the press, which I will take up shortly. Another possibility builds on the traditional FCC policy of encouraging broadcasters to cover local news. This has been a strong ethos of public regulation from the start—and should be even more so today, as local news also withers under financial constraints in the press. By analogy, the FCC should now also require or encourage broadcasters to cover international and global issues. What drove American public policy to stress the coverage of local issues was the concern that the structure and financial incentives of the broadcast press would favor a national rather than a local focus. In a sense, a similar problem now exists with respect to international news. As we saw earlier, one of the most powerful effects of the new communication technologies (especially the Internet) on the traditional press is to undermine the financial wherewithal not to cover international news. This shift is sufficiently problematic that an emphasis on covering international and global news would serve the public interest and be consistent with the traditional goals of public regulation.

Yet another example of how a global free press focus can shift our public policy calibrations involves cable. As we saw earlier in the review of the regulatory system for cable, the industry has achieved some element of journalistic autonomy in shaping the contents of channels sold to subscribers (despite the fact that cable is largely a monopoly medium), while it has also been held appropriate to subject cable operators to various regulations that make them, in effect, common carriers. The "must carry" rule, requiring cable operators to carry the signals of local broadcasters, and the "leased access channel" requirement, which mandates that operators make available a certain number of channels for purchase by prospective content providers, are two prime illustrations of the latter. This system permits a cable operator to decline to carry media such as Al Jazeera in English, as has sometimes happened, out of concern for offending certain portions of its audience base. Given our need to better understand the variety of perspectives emanating from the press in other parts of the world, this is most unfortunate. It would not be so bad if excluded media could turn to the leased access channels to gain access, but the reality is that the process governing that system is highly cumbersome and subject to extensive delays. As such, inappropriate consideration of content is allowed to determine what we can hear. This should be addressed by the cable industry, the FCC, and the courts.

D

The projection outward of the principle of freedom of the press onto the world stage should become a primary goal as we build the rudiments of a global society. Over time in the United States, it should constitute a fourth pillar of the American system of free expression. Already, some of the building blocks of that pillar are clear, as we have seen. It would be most helpful if the Court were to highlight the overall project as such and help us to connect the dots—of discrete cases, doctrines, and discussions—in order to create a narrative of a global public forum with a widely accepted standard of press freedom. What is fundamentally needed is a change in our orientation, characterized by the task of opening up the world to a press that is independent and free.

III

I now want to turn to other ways—consistent with the First Amendment but not mandated by it—by which we might encourage the development of a free press around the world, to achieve in this century on a global stage what the United States created on a national stage in the twentieth century. This will not be easy, in significant part because the mechanisms for breaking down the international regimes of censorship and the barriers to independent journalism are not nearly as clear as they were with an independent judiciary and a constitutional mandate in the First Amendment.

We, therefore, have to find other means to create a global system of freedom of the press. This will require thinking afresh about the myriad ways in which the United States now interacts with the wider world and inventing new ways of doing so. We also have to consider how to build up, sustain, and nurture a press focused on broader global issues. In this final part, I would like to offer some examples of what these might be.

A

First and foremost, we must develop a better system of public funding of the press. I say "better" because our system already has a broad array of public funding mechanisms. Since its creation in 1967 by an act of Congress—which had rejected the idea of a dedicated nonpolitical trust fund supported by a British-style excise tax on television sales—federal appropriations, now some $400 million[22] annually, have flowed directly to the Corporation for Public Broadcasting to PBS, NPR, and approximately 350 public television and 860 public radio stations.[23] Commercial broadcasting effectively operates with public subsidies because it is permitted "free" use of the spectrum,[24] and it is also helped by regulations, such as the requirement that cable operators must carry the signals of local broadcasters.[25] In addition, newspapers and magazines receive financial assistance in indirect ways, for example, through special postal rates and special access to newsworthy events (e.g., presidential press conferences). Nevertheless, there is a perception that the press is not publicly funded and, at least among print journalists, a sense that government funding is antithetical to the spirit of an independent press. This view needs to change, and the whole subject of public funding must be more thoughtfully considered.

The current decline in revenues and profitability of the traditional press, wrought principally by the increasing popularity of the Internet, may become so grave as to require injections of public funds; indeed, my own view is that this will prove to be the only way to sustain a free press over time. But, up to this point, the idea seems to be firmly rejected by most of the press. Additionally, we do not know at this point how this trend will evolve, and there are good arguments for taking a wait-and-see approach. The principal press institutions may yet find ways to stabilize their traditional business model and to improve their profitability through Web sites. Although there is a real risk that the decline will be severe and irreversible, when that becomes apparent there may still be time for public intervention.

The more immediate questions relate to how to facilitate more and better coverage of international news and more participation by the U.S. press in reaching a global audience. Certainly, the decline since the late twentieth century in the capacity of the American press to maintain a deep journalistic presence throughout the world, with the consequence that reporting on international issues has also dropped, is a serious matter. The press now relies more and more heavily on news services, such as the Associated Press and Reuters, which sustain several thousand reporters around the world, and that presence certainly is to be applauded. But there is a need for a rich diversity of reporting sources, arising out of a deep presence in countries and regions across the globe, so that relationships can be nurtured and local knowledge developed.

One clear way to address this issue is to create public funding grants to help finance the operations of foreign bureaus (including the cost of security, which is often a major expense). The obvious concern, of course, is that with government funding will come the risk of government efforts to control the content of journalistic coverage. I will say more about this in a moment, but it is worth bearing in mind that Americans have lived successfully with a variety of major public funding programs in areas where we have a strong interest in maintaining institutional independence. Federal funding of science, the social sciences, international programs, and student scholarships in U.S. colleges and universities is a prime illustration. What makes such programs work is the persistence of universities in maintaining their independence, the watchfulness of the judicial system to block any improper use of funding to control content or to intrude into academic freedom, and the self-restraint of the government. Of equal importance is the way in which grants are awarded, as exemplified by the system of peer review for science funding. Similar structures could easily be developed for grants to the press.

The largest issue, perhaps, is how to encourage a more global footprint for the American press. This process is under way, although to a limited extent. Parts of the press—such as CNN, *Time* and

Newsweek international editions, and the *Wall Street Journal*—already have a substantial international base. Others, such as the *New York Times* and its *International Herald Tribune*, have announced plans to expand their global presence.[26] Web sites provide instantaneous global audiences, although the content is not, by and large, changing as that audience changes. These and other similar plans are important, because they enable others to have the benefits of reporting by an independent and professional American press and because they provide a model for the rest of the world. It is no coincidence that National Public Radio was alone in being able to provide on-the-scene coverage of the devastating 2008 Chengdu earthquake because "All Things Considered" anchors Melissa Block and Robert Seigel were already in the region to produce a series of reports educating American listeners about China.

It should matter to us, too, that the media of other nations—all publicly funded and many actively controlled by the state—are undertaking aggressive plans for establishing a global presence. The BBC, as noted in chapter 3, is far ahead on this. But CCTV, Al Jazeera in English, and other nationally sponsored media are on a similar course. The problem for the American press is, fundamentally, funding. The BBC has the advantage of a steady and very large stream of income coming from the annual fees on television sets (recall that it amounts to well over £3 billion annually).[27] By comparison, American total funding for public television and radio is only a few hundred million dollars.[28] This should change. It would be an enormous improvement in the overall goal of projecting American values around the world to have a vital and responsible press embodied, for example, in the programming of NPR and made available to the world in many languages. The government-funded media that exist in the United States now, from the VOA to the ill-fated Arab-language satellite network, Al Hurra, are either a pale version of what America stands for or completely inconsistent with

America's fundamental values. It would be a better world if the funding for these ventures were reallocated to PBS and NPR to help them develop a strong global presence.

Public broadcasting has occasionally suffered through periods of improper government intrusion into its journalistic autonomy, but on the whole these have been successfully resisted, and there is by now a reasonably solid body of First Amendment decisions that afford protection to institutions receiving federal and state funds. Indeed, it is worth noting that at a time when our fledgling system of public broadcasting was most vulnerable to the direct political and funding threats exerted by the Nixon White House, PBS was the first national network to provide prime-time, gavel-to-gavel coverage of the Watergate hearings in 1973, anchored by new broadcast partners Jim Lehrer and Robert MacNeil. At the same time, Bill Moyers hosted a series of PBS exposes on Watergate and related abuses by the White House. Despite the federal funding it received, the public broadcasting system had already developed the journalistic ethic and independence that provided a model for the commercial network news divisions and ultimately helped bring down the very administration that had sought to undermine its independence.[29]

This is where there is an important role for the courts, using the First Amendment, to establish a principle that public funding not be allowed to compromise editorial independence. For instance, as noted in chapter 1, the Supreme Court has already held that the government cannot constitutionally forbid public broadcasters from expressing editorial viewpoints, even though the government has a legitimate interest in limiting the use of government dollars for such purposes.[30] As with the British system of license fees on television sets, which is not dependent on annual parliamentary appropriations, there are ways to minimize the risks of censorship inherent in public funding. And, given the fact that most of the rest of the world relies on state sponsorship of the press (especially broadcast media) as a means of exercising control over the content of its press, the example of a publicly funded but journalistically independent press would be extremely positive.

This discussion also points to serious constitutional questions about the system of government-operated international broadcast channels. As we have seen, these began in the post–World War II era of fears of the spread of communism. The Voice of America and Radio Free Europe were classic efforts to spread American messages to people vulnerable to communist propaganda.[31] More recently, Al Hurra was added.[32] Although there is an effort in these channels to adhere to standard journalistic values, the fact is that these channels are more concerned with, and are perceived to be concerned with, advancing the agenda of the United States. The very purpose behind the Smith-Mundt Act, which prohibits the rebroadcast of these channels into the United States to protect Americans against U.S. propaganda, is proof of both the basic function of these channels and the serious constitutional problem they present.

There are, as discussed earlier in this chapter, even more aggressive government programs to spread propaganda and to manipulate and exploit foreign media (through bribes, disinformation, and the like) in order to advance U.S. military interests. This kind of activity increased during the wars in Afghanistan and Iraq. Today "cyberwarfare" has become a major focus of defense planners in Washington, D.C., and in other capitals, with the central idea being manipulating the flow of information for strategic advantage. All of these government operations begin to look very different when we think of the United States as being part of a global society, or of trying to move in that direction. We must ask: Would such a government program directed toward U.S. media and citizens violate the First Amendment? We all understand that the government can legitimately advance its policies, whether in the United States or abroad, by honest persuasion. But the deliberate spreading of misinformation and propaganda is another matter. With modern communication technologies, there is no natural border between information distributed abroad and domestically. Information anywhere is information everywhere. That fact, in itself, should lead to grave First Amendment concerns about U.S. disinformation campaigns abroad. We also have the opportunity to announce that, in principle, the foreign press is also the American press in the global society. This, too, should become part of the fourth pillar.

B

It is vital that we focus on the role of international human rights law in helping to develop mechanisms for protecting freedom of the press around the world. The promise of international law should not be understated, yet it is also important to appreciate the challenges to effective enforcement of human rights treaties at the international level and what needs to be done to remedy these gaps. Modern international human rights law has, since its inception in the years following World War II, maintained a strong commitment to freedom of expression and, specifically, to freedom of the press. During its inaugural session in 1946—before any of the modern international human rights treaties were drafted—the United Nations General Assembly passed a resolution recognizing "[f]reedom of information [as] a fundamental human right," which (as noted earlier) is the "touchstone of all the freedoms to which the United Nations is consecrated." Particularly, the assembly recognized that the "right to gather, transmit and publish news anywhere and everywhere" must be at the core of any "serious effort to promote the peace and progress of the world."[33]

The Universal Declaration of Human Rights (UDHR), unanimously adopted by the General Assembly just two years later, built upon this early international commitment to freedom of the press. Although led by Eleanor Roosevelt, the United Nations Commission on Human Rights—the body responsible for drafting the Universal Declaration—was intentionally representative of the membership of the then-nascent United Nations: The first full draft was composed by a Canadian attorney, John Humphrey, and was revised by a French intellectual, René Cassin, with significant input from Dr. P. C. Chang, a representative from China, and Charles Malik of Lebanon.[34] To facilitate even greater consensus, the commission proposed a declaration, leaving for another day the task of drafting and ratifying a binding treaty.[35] Many have argued, however, that given the near-universal acceptance of the Universal Declaration, at least some of its provisions have attained the status of customary international law.[36] In other words, even though treaties that have embedded the Universal Declaration into positive legal obligations are binding only on those nations that have formally ratified these conventions, all countries—even those that are not members of the United Nations—may now be bound by it.

It is also worth noting that, although the intellectual origins of modern human rights can be traced to the natural rights theories of the Enlightenment, the drafters of the Universal Declaration avoided references to the Western philosophical tradition as part of their effort to universalize the rights contained in the document. Furthermore, this emphasis on enunciating a global norm affected the way that the rights were formulated.[37] Rather than conceptualizing the right to freedom of speech and freedom of the press as a necessary check on government power in a constitutional democracy, for example, freedom of expression in the Universal Declaration focuses on the individual's right to know or to "seek, receive, and impart information."[38]

The provision of the Universal Declaration of Human Rights protecting "freedom of expression" was incorporated, almost verbatim, into the text of the International Covenant on Civil and Political Rights (ICCPR)—one of the two binding treaties implementing the international human rights system envisioned by the Universal

Declaration. Virtually the same language was used in both the American Convention on Human Rights and the European Convention for the Protection of Human Rights and Fundamental Freedoms.[39] This reflects an extraordinary consensus in major international legal instruments about the principle of freedom of the press.

The relevant part of Article 19 of the International Covenant on Civil and Political Rights provides that "[e]veryone shall have the right to freedom of expression; this right shall include freedom to seek, receive, and impart information and ideas of all kinds, regardless of frontiers, either orally, in writing or in print, in the form of art, or through any other media of his choice." Four concepts embedded within this provision merit consideration. First, the right to "seek" and "receive" information and ideas has increasingly been viewed as a right to information held by public authorities—similar to the right of access that I endorsed earlier in the domestic context.[40]

Second, the United Nations Human Rights Committee—the body responsible for expounding the meaning of the International Covenant on Civil and Political Rights and addressing alleged violations of the treaty—has found that the "information and ideas of any kind" provision encompasses every form of idea and opinion, including news and information, commercial expression, and works of art. Moreover, "it should not be confined to means of political, cultural or artistic expression."[41] However, this generous reading of Article 19 has been qualified by several explicit limitations that may render the International Convenant of Civil and Political Rights' right to free expression less protective than the First Amendment.

Article 19 expressly limits the right to freedom of expression by stating that the rights guaranteed in the article "carr[y]...special duties and responsibilities" and "may therefore be subject to certain restrictions...as are provided by law and are necessary: (a) For respect of the rights or reputations of others; (b) For the protection of national security or of public order [*ordre public*], or of public health or morals." An additional limit on free expression, contained in Article 20, not only permits but requires nations to prohibit war propaganda and "advocacy of national, racial or religious hatred that constitutes incitement to discrimination, hostility or violence."

Third, Article 19 of both the Universal Declaration of Human Rights and the International Covenant on Civil and Political Rights explicitly states that the right to freedom of expression has extraterritorial implications: An individual's right to information exists "regardless of frontiers." Within the context of the larger body of international human rights law, this phrase is unique. The general presumption is that a nation is responsible only for ensuring the human rights of its citizens and those within its territory,[42] but Article 19 suggests that citizens of one nation may have a right against other nations. As early as 1948, long before the advent of the Internet, the drafters of the Universal Declaration recognized that some sort of international framework would be essential for protecting the right to freedom of expression in an increasingly interconnected world.

Finally, Article 2 of the International Convenant of Civil and Political Rights, which establishes the treaty's operative principles, requires every party to the treaty "to respect and ensure...the rights recognized." Like the conceptualization of freedom of expression as the "right to know" rather than merely as a right to speak, this provision acknowledges that protecting freedom of expression imposes both positive and negative obligations on nations. For example, the International Covenant on Civil and Political Rights has been interpreted to create an affirmative duty to respond to the "development of modern mass media" by implementing "effective measures...necessary to prevent such control of the media as would interfere with the right of everyone to freedom of expression."[43]

Though less than perfect, the right to free expression embodied in international human rights law has much to recommend it. As we have seen, the scope of the right is largely consistent with and in some ways expands upon the First Amendment. Perhaps even more important, 164 nations are now parties to the International Covenant of Civil and Political Rights.[44] We have, therefore, a foundation on which to build and nurture a strong and vital global principle of freedom of the press.

But the real meaning of any legal norm cannot be understood without considering the mechanisms for enforcement, and here, unfortunately, the barriers to effective implementation remain significant. The International Covenant on Civil and Political Rights and the Optional Protocol establish two primary institutional channels for international enforcement: country reports and individual communications.[45] Although different in some respects, these provisions share two limitations: They require governments' cooperation to facilitate the review process, and they do not grant the reviewing body the authority to sanction nations for noncompliance.

At the time of ratification and every five years thereafter, Article 40 of the International Covenant on Civil and Political Rights requires parties to the treaty to submit country reports to the Human Rights Committee (HRC) on the measures they have adopted to give effect to the rights recognized in the treaty. Additionally, since the early 1990s, the committee has "occasionally requested states to submit 'emergency' reports when 'recent or current events [indicated] that the enjoyment of [ICCPR] rights [had] been seriously affected' in the nation."[46] In addition to spelling out this basic reporting obligation, Article 40 establishes a review process, authorizing the committee to "study the reports" and to issue concluding observations. These are not, however, binding in any legal sense.

Although the reporting process lacks any legal consequences, the Committee often works with international civil society to develop political pressure to implement its recommendations. When conducting a review, the committee can consider both the report prepared by the nation and "shadow reports" prepared by international and domestic human rights organizations. Depending on the human rights conditions in the reporting nation, human rights groups can then use the review process as an opportunity to engage in a constructive dialogue with the nation's government or to shame the government by drawing international media attention to ongoing abuses.[47] Still, despite this development, periodic reports remain a weak means of enforcing the International Convenant of Civil and Political Rights. The reports are notoriously late (Gambia's report was twenty-one years "overdue" in 2006), and countries that are responsible for the most egregious human rights violations often do not respond to public pressures, especially in the absence of any threat of concrete punitive action.[48]

The final method for enforcement at the international level is the individual communication, which was established by the Optional Protocol to the International Covenant on Civil and Political Rights. Approximately two-thirds of the parties to the International Convenant of Civil and Political Rights have ratified this supplemental instrument.[49] (While the United States signed the International Convenant of Civil and Political Rights in 1977 and ratified it in 1992, it has not signed nor ratified the Optional Protocol.) The Optional Protocol empowers the Human Rights Committee to review individual complaints. But, even when considering such cases, the Committee operates under significant practical limitations: It lacks the power to conduct fact finding; it cannot take testimony; and it does not hear arguments from the parties.[50] Additionally, the Committee is authorized only to issue its findings, which lack formal legal authority under international law.[51]

The Human Rights Committee has taken several steps to increase its authority to hear claims and to promote the authority of its "views." It has developed a "default judgment jurisprudence" to prevent states from failing to respond to communications. This doctrine has proven especially significant when only the government has access to the information that would be necessary for the committee to reach a legal conclusion.[52] The Committee has also self-consciously imbued its decisions with legal reasoning and has "become quite outspoken in its view that defending states are under an obligation to comply with unfavorable decisions against them." Finally, the committee has even "taken concrete steps to monitor compliance, appointing one of its members as a special rapporteur to record states' responses."[53]

These are necessary steps, but without more they are insufficient. In 1995, the Committee's rapporteur to assess compliance with the committee's views found that only 30 percent of the nations that responded to his request for follow-up information had performed "satisfactor[ily]," meaning that they "displayed a willingness...to implement the Committee's Views or to offer the applicant an appropriate remedy."[54] A 2006 report of the rapporteur's findings noted that many nations "have failed to implement the Views adopted under the Optional Protocol."[55] Perhaps even more important, the committee continues to lack the authority to hear individual complaints against the countries that have chosen not to sign the protocol, including the United States, the United Kingdom, China, and India.

In contrast to the weak enforcement associated with the Human Rights Committee's reporting and communications procedures, the European Court of Human Rights and the Inter-American Court of Human Rights have been notable for achieving a greater degree of compliance with their decisions.[56] Regional treaties enforced by these courts contain provisions that are similar to the text of the International Covenant on Civil and Political Rights. Indeed, up to this point, the regional conventions have achieved the greatest level of legal effectiveness.

The United States should ratify the American Convention on Human Rights and submit to the jurisdiction of the Inter-American Court of Human Rights. Only after the United States has agreed to abide by the court's holdings will it be in a position to encourage others to conform to the court's judgments. In our interdependent world, these judgments are not only for the benefit of citizens of other nations, they are also needed to protect the rights of Americans. As we have seen, national borders cannot contain the dangers confronting the American press. It is in the U.S. national self-interest for these rights to be protected internationally. To this end, the United States must recommit itself to the expansion of the international principle of freedom of expression that it helped to establish more than sixty years ago. The United States must be prepared to make itself subject to international oversight, including by ratifying the Optional Protocol to the International Convenant of Civil and Political Rights. The United States and other like-minded nations should join in the Human Rights Committee's effort to make the views in individual communications proceedings legally binding and to build upon the committee's default judgment doctrine by voluntarily permitting the Committee to engage in greater fact finding than is currently authorized by the Optional Protocol. Most important, the United States should make good-faith efforts to remedy treaty violations identified by the committee and should urge other nations to do the same.

In sum, the norms at the core of international human rights law are largely consistent with the traditional conception of the First Amendment. If properly developed, these ideas could help to provide the base for legal protection of freedom of the press in the twenty-first century. The challenge is to capture this potential by creating a system of enforcement capable of bringing these ideas to life. To be sure, there are problems we will have to confront over some issues involving the scope of these rights. With respect to freedom of speech and press, for example, there is significant support across the world for restrictions on expression that incites "hatred" on the basis of such categories as religion and race, which (as we have seen) has been firmly rejected by the Supreme Court. Nevertheless, bearing in mind the importance of building a foundation for a free and independent press in the emerging global society, it is preferable to agree on the general norms and to employ reservations and declarations—statements filed at the time of ratification that exempt parties from compliance with specific provisions or limit enforcement to particular interpretations—to help address these secondary concerns.

C

While international and regional treaties guarantee freedom of expression but offer too few structures for implementing this value and ensuring compliance, international trade and investment laws lack the express articulation of the norm but provide robust methods of enforcement. An interesting but underdeveloped issue is whether there are possibilities for a convergence of the two regimes.

One possible avenue is in the realm of international trade. The World Trade Organization (WTO) is the multilateral regime that governs its 153 member countries' trade activities.[57] It could potentially be used to uphold the freedom of expression principles that are enshrined in separate international agreements, such as the Universal Declaration of Human Rights and the International Covenant on Civil and Political Rights. Regional and bilateral trade agreements, such as the North American Free Trade Agreement (NAFTA) and the U.S.–Peru Trade Promotion Agreement, could serve a similar purpose. The overarching goal would be to use trade sanctions to compel trading partners to adhere to the freedom of expression principles to which they have committed in nontrade agreements. But, as is always the case, the main shift required is in our thinking—namely, in understanding that a free press is a necessary condition to any sustainable free trade relationship.

This is, not unexpectedly, a controversial proposition. Some members of the WTO (mainly, developing countries) have long resisted the addition of a "social clause" in trade agreements, which might allow policy concerns such as labor rights and the environment to be linked to trade through the multilateral trade system.[58] Moreover, the European Union and Canada have led the opposition to liberalization of trade in the "culture" or media sector.[59] For example, the General Agreement on Tariffs and Trade (GATT) contained an exception in Article IV that permitted screen quotas for films in order to allow the fledgling European domestic cinema to compete against the industry in the United States.[60] This provision was included at the behest of France. However, during the 1980s, when cultural flows increased and trade in television programs was on the rise, the United States argued that Article IV should be construed narrowly to exclude television—meaning that American television programs should be allowed the same access to foreign markets as domestic television broadcasters have. The dispute was never resolved.[61]

During negotiations for the General Agreement on Trade in Services (GATS), the European Union and Canada pushed to exclude "audiovisual services" (meaning motion pictures and television broadcasts). Although no such official exemption was made, there is a de facto exemption for audiovisual services, since under the agreement countries can choose the sectors where they grant market access, or agree to "national treatment," and the EU and Canadian restrictions on television and film broadcasts continue in force.[62] ("National treatment" in the WTO requires countries not to discriminate between foreign and domestic goods and services.)[63] As discussed in chapter 3, Canada and the European Union have policies mandating a certain amount of domestic content in television and radio broadcasts.

Disputes over domestic content quotas have arisen in other trade contexts as well, and sometimes negotiations lead to greater openness. For example, South Korea agreed to restrictions on its screen quota system (designed to ensure that Korean cinemas broadcast a certain amount of domestic films) as a precondition to negotiating its free-trade agreement with the United States.[64]

The general question whether outright political censorship falls under the system of the WTO has been avoided by its appellate body, out of a general sense that "censorship was not meant to be considered a trade barrier" under the GATT or the GATS.[65] Nevertheless, there remains considerable potential for invoking the market-access provisions of the WTO, the principle of national treatment, and the system of international trade law generally in order to improve opportunities for the development of a free and independent press around the world. In the evolution of First Amendment jurisprudence, censorship and discriminatory (or, inversely, favorable) treatment of certain segments of the press (e.g., through selective taxation) came to be seen as fundamentally incompatible with the needs of democracy and a free market economy. The same perspective could take hold in the realm of international trade. Information, not just a particular "good" or "service," is the life blood of these systems. In fact, a few cases have come to the WTO dispute resolution system using the classic free-trade language of market access and national treatment rather than the language of freedom of the press, but the effects are the same.

For example, the United States brought to the WTO a trade dispute with Canada over the right of a U.S. magazine to publish in Canada. When *Sports Illustrated* began producing a split-run version of its magazine, which was printed in Canada, it ran afoul of a Canadian excise tax that was meant to protect domestic magazines and to ensure at least 80 percent Canadian content. The United States argued that this tax constituted discrimination against foreign producers and violated the WTO's national treatment standard. In 1997, the WTO appellate body (which is charged with interpreting WTO "law" and issuing legal decisions) ruled in favor of the United States.[66] This trade victory constituted a blow against cultural protectionist measures, with significant implications for freedom of expression and the ability of outside media to enter a country.

A case filed in the WTO by the United States against China over the Xinhua News Agency also raised the issue of trade barriers affecting American media companies. China had enacted rules in 2006 empowering Xinhua to "regulate news services that distribute financial information in China, effectively barring foreign financial news providers from soliciting Chinese subscribers directly."[67] Again, the dispute was couched in the terminology of trade violations rather than explicitly addressing free press concerns. The United States argued that Xinhua's monopoly over regulation and the policy of barring foreign media from the Chinese market violated WTO rules on national treatment and market access. The U.S. Trade Representative (USTR) Susan Schwab said, "China's restrictive treatment of outside suppliers of financial information services places U.S. and other foreign suppliers at a serious competitive disadvantage."[68] The two countries eventually reached a settlement with China agreeing to employ an independent regulator for financial information services and to make its licensing requirements fair and transparent.[69]

In still another case, in April 2007, the USTR objected to China's policies in the audiovisual sector. The United States pointed out that China "limits the right to import reading materials, [audiovisual home entertainment] products, sound recordings, and films for theatrical release to certain Chinese state-owned enterprises," thereby excluding foreign enterprises from importing such goods. The United States argued that these measures were inconsistent with the market access and national treatment commitments that China made in the GATS, among other trade violations.[70] In August 2009, the WTO publicly circulated the panel report ruling in favor of the United States, finding that China must lift import restrictions and ease distribution rules for copyrighted works. The U.S. Trade Representative Ron Kirk deemed the decision a "significant victory to America's creative industries."[71]

In the summer of 2009, another controversy erupted when China announced that it would require all personal computers imported into and sold in the country to be fitted with Internet-filtering software known as Green Dam-Youth Escort. The Chinese government claims that the purpose behind the requirement is to block children's access to pornographic sites, but there is widespread concern and belief that the government will use the software to censor political information. This prompted traditional human rights and business groups to object strenuously, but interestingly both the U.S. Secretary of Commerce Gary Locke and U.S. Trade Representative Kirk also raised objections invoking China's obligations under the WTO agreement. The letter of protest they sent to the Chinese government was not immediately made public, but in a statement released at the time Mr. Locke wrote that "China is putting companies in an untenable position by requiring them, with virtually no public notice, to preinstall software that appears to have broad-based censorship implications and network security issues." Without seeing the formal letter sent to the Chinese, it is difficult to identify precisely the grounds of the trade complaint. There are several possibilities. A very modest basis would be that companies were given inadequate time to prepare to meet the new filtering requirement. A stronger claim would be that the filter requirement disadvantaged foreign producers over Chinese companies. The most interesting and an important possibility, however, is the inclusion of concerns—in the context of trade—about the potential for impermissible censorship. What we should hope and aim for, however, is not simply a generalized concern, coming out of the free trade community, about censorship, but a commitment to and belief in the principle that effective free trade cannot happen in an environment of such censorship, especially not in the absence of a free and independent press. The logic of this perspective would lead to objections to unacceptable censorship of all kinds, not only censorship stemming from particular product requirements that might facilitate some forms of censorship. On July 1, 2009, the date China had initially given for equipping personal computers with filters, it announced that it was postponing the regulation, and then in August 2009, the government appeared to back down from the requirement entirely, releasing a statement saying the software would not have to be made available with new computers.[72]

The law of international trade, including its system of strong enforcement, offers interesting possibilities for achieving free press objectives, and more should be done to explore this potential. But there is another area with at least equal potential to further the value of freedom of the press, namely, the elaborate system of agreements throughout the world that govern private foreign investment. In terms of scale, this latter system is twice as large as global trade in goods and services. The purpose of the approximately 2,600 treaties currently in force—referred to as bilateral investment treaties, or BITs—is to protect foreign investments from interference by the host government. If abridged, the common treaty provision permits the private investor to seek damages against the host government through binding arbitration—unlike trade agreements, which typically only permit state-to-state enforcement claims. The United States is party to about 50 investment treaties.[73]

The system governing global economic relations has grown exponentially since the early to mid-1990s, and it has the potential to become an effective lever in dealing with free press issues on a global scale. The BITs typically contain provisions calling for compensation for breaches of general international investment law principles, such as "fair and equitable treatment," "denial of justice," "full protection and security," "most-favored nation treatment," and "national treatment."[74] As is true in the international trade context generally, BITs typically do not protect freedom of expression (although they very well could), but the treaty provisions may nonetheless guard against government action that has the effect of curtailing expression. There have already been several cases brought to international arbitration that involve the broadcast and print media and publishing industries. There have been disputes over the denial of broadcast licenses and over government censorship of media companies for voicing criticisms of the host state.[75]

In one pending case, a U.S. investor alleged that Ukraine arbitrarily denied it broadcasting licenses, in violation of the "fair and equal treatment" principle.[76] This dispute is another instance of domestic content quotas having trade implications, as the restrictions (which required a minimum percentage of local music on the air) were introduced after the U.S. investor entered the field, barring full competition. In another case against Ukraine, a Lithuanian investor claimed to have been harassed for publishing material for a political opposition party. Although the arbitral tribunal did not find harassment amounting to a breach of the treaty, it indicated that such forms of harassment (punishing a foreign publisher for "its impertinence in printing materials opposed to the [governing] regime") might constitute a violation of investment treaty provisions in a future case.[77]

Another very novel but potentially important idea is to argue for a "right of establishment" by using BITs that provide that foreign investors be treated no less well than domestic investors (i.e., national treatment). On this theory, especially when the provision applies to domestic investments prior to the BIT, foreign media can claim that the treaty gives them a right to establish themselves in the host country and to be free of special censorship regimes, provided that equivalent domestic media can be owned privately. It is worth noting that multilateral free-trade agreements, such as NAFTA, have chapters on investment which also can be helpful in these ways.[78]

These trade and investment treaty cases demonstrate the potential for freedom of the press principles to be enforced through the multilateral trade and investment regimes. This possibility further highlights the importance of having a global norm of freedom of the press, one that all trading countries could be said generally to share. It also shows that countries, and specifically the United States, need to become more focused on and explicit about the link between freedom of expression and trade and to recognize how curbs on speech and press can be detrimental to free trade.

I hope that the U.S. trade representative will pursue the connection between trade and freedom of communication. For too long, free press and human rights concerns have been largely left to the realm of the State Department. In 2007, however, Google appealed for help from U.S. trade authorities, with Google's director of public policy and government affairs stating that it is "fair to say that censorship is the No. 1 barrier to trade that we face." In response, the USTR said that, if "censorship regimes create barriers to trade in violation of international trade rules, the USTR would get involved."[79]

It is also noteworthy that, in December 2007, an organization called the California First Amendment Coalition (CFAC) petitioned the USTR to file a case against China in the World Trade Organization to force China to end its Internet censorship. The CFAC argued that international trade laws should be used to address Internet access and censorship problems, an issue never before considered by the WTO. The CFAC described its effort as follows:

> Our (concededly novel) theory: that China's censorship of the internet, the most pervasive and systematic system of censorship in the world, violates China's obligations under treaties it signed (the GATT, covering free trade in goods, and the GATS, covering services) in order to join the WTO. We contend China must end its censorship or risk limitations on its access to US markets.[80]

Interestingly, the CFAC petition also mentioned that China's Internet filtering violated Article 19 of the UDHR and Article 19 of the International Covenant on Civil and Political Rights,[81] explicitly connecting freedom of expression and free trade.

The USTR has not indicated whether it will pursue the CFAC's case against China in the World Trade Organization.[82] But despite the limited engagement of the USTR and the WTO on the issue, there is growing acceptance around the world of treating Internet censorship as a trade barrier, subject to the laws and enforcement mechanisms of various bilateral and multilateral trade regimes.[83] The European Parliament recently launched an initiative to treat Internet censorship as a trade barrier in response to companies such as Google, Yahoo, Telecom Italia, and France Telecom facing censorship in China.[84] It remains to be seen whether this initiative will be successful and whether censorship of other media will be treated as a trade barrier as well.

The USTR could similarly assert that direct and indirect obstacles to freedom of expression (whether censorship, licensing restrictions, or other measures) constitute actionable trade violations. This would help to protect freedom of expression in specific instances. But, even more important, as with the Supreme Court and the First Amendment in the United States, it would contribute to the creation of a global principle of freedom of the press by visibly upholding it and defining what activities should be protected. Just as the United States has come to embrace concerns over the environment and labor standards as key elements of its free trade and investment relationships around the world, so too should it incorporate the values of freedom of speech and press.

D

America's graduate-level journalism schools could be a major lever to help prepare journalists, from the United States and abroad, for an increasingly integrated global society. At the present time, these schools collectively educate about 4,000 students per year, about 2.5 percent of the total number of journalists in the United States.[85]

Most, perhaps all, of these schools also offer continuing-education programs for practicing journalists. Foreign journalists and international students also come to the United States to study. Of the approximately 600,000 international students in the United States each year,[86] approximately 9,200 (or 1.5 percent) are involved in communications and journalism programs.[87] Finally, American journalism schools increasingly are offering programs in other countries around the world, making it easier for U.S. students to have international experiences and for students overseas to study journalism. Some schools are involved in helping other countries to establish their own programs and schools for training journalists.

Whenever the United States has wanted to make significant advances in knowledge or in its preparedness for increased understanding about the world, the nation has relied upon government programs and funding. This is most vividly and successfully illustrated in the realm of scientific research, and it has also been true in U.S. efforts to improve knowledge about the international arena. In the era after World War II, the federal government began funding regional and area studies programs at universities (including language instruction) along with programs to support international students.[88] Now, we should extend these programs to journalism education.

Journalism schools are improving. Historically, they have been among the weaker academic programs in universities. Some are mere vocational programs, teaching students how to do what they will do on their first day of work as reporters. Others have focused on the theoretical study of systems of mass communication. For in-depth inquiry into politics, economics, science, or culture, most journalism schools have sent their students to other departments for general courses on those subjects. The idea that journalism is a profession and that a journalism school in a university should be structured in order to educate future members of the profession and to interact with the field in the ways that other professional schools do—most notably, law and medicine—has not been realized.

There are many reasons that this has been so. Journalism students cannot look forward to earning high salaries upon graduation, which puts pressure on schools to abbreviate the time before the awarding of degrees and to stress practical skills rather than deeper knowledge that will sustain journalists over the course of their careers. This is a fixable problem, primarily by expanding financial aid to students in the same way we do in other fields (e.g., graduate study in the humanities) where we want to sustain knowledge and expertise over time even though the market does not generously reward people who pursue these studies.

The primary reason, though, is substantive: Journalism schools must develop the content, or knowledge, needed by professionals devoted to reporting on what is happening in the world. As our reliance on the press to understand the world has increased, so too has the need for journalists to have the substantive knowledge to perform that function. To be sure, this is not inconsistent with a strong professional education designed to teach students the practical skills they need to function effectively. Medicine trains future doctors how to perform operations, and law schools offer students the opportunity to practice in legal clinics. But, over many decades, both of these professional schools have moved from that kind of training to recognizing and building a body of knowledge appropriate to the profession that students should learn and be immersed in. Journalism education, on the whole, has yet to make this transformation. The questions are: What should a student aiming to be a journalist at the highest level know upon graduation, and how should a journalism school structure such an educational program? Presumably, this should include substantial knowledge about, for example, the global economic system. But appropriate knowledge about economics for a journalism student is different from what is appropriate for students focusing on economics, law, business, or history. We need to reform the American system of journalism education to meet the needs of journalists of the future.

At the Columbia Graduate School of Journalism, under the imaginative leadership of Nicholas Lemann as dean, the faculty has made significant progress in this direction. Supplementing the traditional one-year program, which emphasizes practical journalistic skills, a new optional second-year program focusing on areas of substantive knowledge and expertise has been introduced (supported by a strong financial aid system). This is a signal development in the improvement of journalism education. At the same time, like other schools, the Columbia journalism school is putting greater emphasis on educating students for a new media environment characterized by new technologies and an increased global focus.

Journalism schools should be a primary focus of national policy for generating a free and independent press in the United States and around the world. Nothing exceeds the power of a great education to change the way people think. It would be enormously beneficial to bring journalists, practicing and aspiring, from all over the world to learn together in the exhilarating environment of America's great universities. As I have traveled and met with journalists, I have never met one who did not want to be able to work in a free press such as has been created in the United States. Nothing could nurture and fortify the profession of journalism in the new global society more than a well-funded system of journalism schools, led by those in American universities.

E

This discussion of ways to go about creating a free press for the twenty-first century is hardly exhaustive. Not only are there other levers that may be useful now, but new ones will emerge in the years ahead. Here are just a few additional areas to be considered:

(a) It matters what national leaders say. I have talked about the courts, and especially the Supreme Court, and how the decisions they reach and the opinions they write about freedom of the press affect national and international cultures. The same is true of the president and other political leaders. We need fewer of the traditional perorations on human rights and more hard-headed analyses of the critical role of meaningful flows of information in an increasingly integrated and pluralistic globe. The message to countries with regimes of very restrictive press control should be that the United States cannot continue building an economic relationship without the openness that only a free press can provide; this is at least as significant as the transparency of common accounting practices.

(b) It matters in getting other countries to open up to American journalists what U.S. policy is toward their journalists. Visa and accreditation policies, for example, can have a very significant impact on the development of a free press both in the United States and around the world. One noteworthy instance involves Iran: Under current U.S. policy, there are few Iranian journalists in the country, and just one is accredited to the United Nations, which permits travel only within a twenty-five mile radius of New York.[89] Britain, on the other hand, has dozens of Iranian journalists based in London. As a consequence, there are far fewer American journalists and press bureaus allowed to operate within Iran, while British journalists and media regularly are. (*The Washington Post*, for example, has to rely on a Dutch newspaper correspondent as its stringer in Iran because it is not allowed to open a separate bureau there.) The more general point is that every U.S. policy should be evaluated for its impact on sustaining and advancing freedom of the press throughout the world.

To be sure, there is a national security interest in protecting against other countries using the cover of "journalists" for spying and intelligence gathering purposes. Yet, from the standpoint of the basic principle of freedom of the press, we know that national security interests are often inflated at the expense of the principle and, in any case, do not necessarily trump free press interests. The government should at least feel compelled to exhaust all other reasonable means of meeting our security needs. That's what the *Pentagon Papers* and other cases teach.

(c)   It matters whether the U.S. government uses its leverage in the conduct of foreign policy to try to secure access for the press. I have repeatedly heard experts in international trade law and policy lament the low level of understanding in the press about these complex issues. The Clinton administration made special efforts in various major trade negotiations to secure greater involvement for the press. This is clearly an important and valuable effort.

(d)   It is vital that we recognize how important a free press is to achieving other goals and that we shape U.S. policies in light of this recognition. This is the point emphasized earlier when I noted the observation by Paul Collier about the crucial role a free press can perform in making international aid effective in dealing with the billion people living in extreme poverty. The same is true of international trade policies, as we have seen, and of military actions to secure the peace. It is natural for government departments to become overly focused on their discrete objectives—leaving trade to Commerce and democracy promotion to State—but it is necessary to overcome this tendency when it is clear that a broader and more integrated perspective will help to realize America's broader goals.

(e)   We need to keep an eye out for opportunities to advance the cause of a free press by using it as a condition in negotiations for other, perhaps seemingly distinct, relationships. The European Union has been reasonably effective in getting countries seeking admission to embrace more robust laws and policies for freedom of speech and press. The 2008 Summer Olympics held in Beijing was another example of an opportunity to achieve greater global commitments to the principles of freedom of the press and speech. As part of China's commitments for hosting the summer Olympics, the government promised in 2002 to "be open in every respect."[90] Following the games, it announced that the "easing of restrictions on foreign journalists enacted for the Olympics would become permanent." As reported by the *New York Times*, "[u]nder the new rules, foreign reporters do not need government permission to travel within China or to interview its citizens."[91] Although it made it virtually impossible for Chinese citizens to engage in public protests following the games, the government announced that the "easing of restrictions on foreign journalists enacted for the Olympics would become permanent." Whether China will, in fact, revert to its pre-Olympics system of censorship is currently a matter of debate, and certainly the closing of Tibet to the press is a widely noted and alarming retrenchment. However, just to take one example, the BBC World Service's Chinese online site, launched in 1999 and comprehensively blocked by the Chinese government until just before the Olympics, is now only selectively blocked, such that the home page and international news pages are generally available, although some stories on China or Taiwan are precluded.

(f)   We need more effective ways to advocate for a global free press. The methods by which we define a nation's well-being, for example, are being rethought, and people's access to information and ideas is surely an important element of a good life, yet it is not included in measures such as GDP or GNP.

(g) We need a nuanced view of how countries exert control and censorship of the press, and we need to use this understanding to find ways to minimize these influences. For example, state control over the Internet is often facilitated by having only one Internet service provider, so being alert to opportunities to insist on more than one could be very helpful.

(h) One way of protecting journalists from unofficial but systemic violence, which can cause all of the problems of official censorship, is for countries to enact laws specifically prohibiting and punishing these crimes. In Mexico, for example, following the appalling wave of attacks on members of the press, President Felipe Calderón's administration proposed legislation making "attacks against journalists...federal crimes and...[making] federal authorities responsible for the investigation of these crimes."[92] The law would also "create a special justice department office that would investigate attacks and killings that threaten freedom of expression" and would raise the sentences of persons convicted of these crimes.[93]

(i) I have already spoken about journalism schools and the role they should assume in promoting a free press around the world. But my own field of law can also play a role, especially if it broadens its focus. Every law school has courses on freedom of speech and press, yet the content is almost entirely about U.S. constitutional case law. Many graduates of American law schools emerge very knowledgeable about the First Amendment and what it has come to mean. But law school casebooks rarely treat the subject of building a free press for a global society. New generations of law students must begin to think about a free press in this broader perspective. It is also important that other fields of law—international trade law, for example—become integrated into these discussions.

There are undoubtedly many more approaches we can pursue, but the key points are these: Creating a free press for a global society, one that is "uninhibited, robust, and wide-open," can happen only if we make it a central priority. We must see its relevance to our other fundamental goals. We must take the long view, because it will take time to achieve these goals, just as it took the United States a century, in fits and starts, to bring the First Amendment to where it is today. A global society is the ultimate pluralistic society, with many disparate voices that need to be heard, and tolerance for dissent and disagreement must be learned. A change in how we see the world is necessary for our future, and a free press will help to facilitate that change.

Epilogue

WORKING ON THIS BOOK has been a voyage of discovery for me, opening up new dimensions of freedom of the press I had not considered before. I have come to appreciate that the greatest threat to a free press in today's world is not the financial crisis that afflicts so much of the media, particularly newspapers, but the national and international barriers to gathering and reporting the news, which become more serious every day as our need for quality journalism becomes more global. Coming as I do with a long-standing relationship to the First Amendment, it is perhaps natural to want to begin to project this extraordinary system onto the world at large. To be sure, the complexities in this undertaking are enormous. Given the design of this book, I have focused on the need for and the basic elements of that effort rather than the dilemmas of scaling up, as it were. But extensive study of the latter is obviously required.

It is also important to acknowledge that the world is made up of very different views about how to live and how to organize societies, not least about freedom of the press. To project a U.S. free press system onto the world may seem to some as just another instance of Americans' insensitivity to global differences. To this, I offer three responses. First, it is always important to bear in mind that a system of free expression is the means—the *medium*—by which all human beings will best understand, accommodate, and learn to respect or resolve these vast differences. In this way, the principle of freedom of the press (and speech) is distinctive. Second, the more people to whom I talk around the world about issues of freedom of speech and press, the more I am impressed by how much consensus there actually is for these norms. Violations are all too frequent, but they often occur with rationalizations that, while dubious in logic, are consistent with a tacit acceptance of the norm itself. And, as I argued in chapter 4, there is certainly a strong base of international laws, customs, and organizations devoted to freedom of the press upon which we can build. Finally, it needs to be emphasized, again, that what is at stake here is not imposing an American view of rights on others solely for their sake but rather trying to secure what we believe that the United States, as well as the world, needs to live successfully with globalization.

This book has looked at the problem of what must be done for a global free press from a U.S. perspective. But we need to do this from the vantage point of other countries as well, especially those that generally share the same philosophy about the importance of a free and independent press. A collective effort toward the same end is a necessity.

Notes

CHAPTER 1

1. Geoffrey R. Stone et al., Constitutional Law 1050 (5th ed. 2005).

2. Id.

3. Id.

4. Potter Stewart, "Or of the Press," 26 Hastings L.J. 631, 633 (1975).

5. Id.

6. Id. at 634.

7. 435 U.S. 765 (1978).

8. Id. at 797–99.

9. Id. at 801–2.

10. 301 U.S. 103, 123 (1937).

11. Id. at 125.

12. Id. at 132–33.

13. Minneapolis Star & Tribune Co. v. Minnesota Commissioner of Revenue, 460 U.S. 575, 577–78 (1983).

14. Id. at 588–89.

15. Id. at 591.

16. Id. at 598.

17. Arkansas Writers' Project, Inc. v. Ragland, 481 U.S. 221, 228 (1987).

18. 395 U.S. 444, 448–49 (1969).

19. Id. at 447.

20. See, e.g., Morse v. Frederick, 127 S. Ct. 2618, 2650 (2007) ("Our First Amendment jurisprudence has identified some categories of expression that are less deserving of protection than others—fighting words, obscenity, and commercial speech, to name a few").

21. 376 U.S. 254 (1964).

22. Id. at 256; Heed Their Rising Voices, N.Y. Times, Mar. 29, 1960, at L25, available at http://1stam.umn.edu/archive/primary/sullivan.pdf.

23. Sullivan, 376 U.S. at 258, 265.

24. Id. at 257–58.

25. Id. at 260 n.3.

26. Id. at 258–59.

27. Id. at 256.

28. Id. at 270.

29. Id. at 271–76.

30. Id. at 273–74.

31. Id. at 276. The act permitted the defendant to escape punishment if he or she could prove the truth of what was said. Id. at 273.

32. Id. at 279.

33. Id. at 295 (Black, J., concurring).

34. Id. at 297 (Goldberg, J., concurring) (quoting id. at 262 (majority opinion)).

35. Id. at 287–88 (majority opinion).

36. 418 U.S. 323 (1974).

37. Id. at 345.

38. Id. at 350.

39. Harry Kalven, Jr., The *New York Times* Case: A Note on "the Central Meaning of the First Amendment," 1964 Sup. Ct. Rev. 191, 208–9.

40. Samuel D. Warren & Louis D. Brandeis, The Right to Privacy, 4 Harv. L. Rev. 193, 196 (1890).

41. Id.

42. 420 U.S. 469 (1975).

43. Id. at 472–74.

44. Id. at 491.

45. 491 U.S. 542, 532 (1989).

46. 532 U.S. 514, 535 (2001).

47. N.Y. Times Co. v. U.S. (*Pentagon Papers Case*), 403 U.S. 713 (1971).

48. Brief of the United States at 2–3, id. (Nos. 1873 and 1875).

49. Id. at 13–21.

50. See Martin Arnold, *Pentagon Papers* Charges Are Dismissed; Judge Byrne Frees Ellsberg and Russo, N.Y. Times, May 12, 1973, at A1.

51. *Pentagon Papers Case*, at 717 (Black, J., concurring).

52. Id. at 724 (Douglas, J., concurring) (quoting *Sullivan*).

53. Id. at 726–27 (Brennan, J., concurring).

54. Id. at 730 (Stewart, J., concurring); see also id. at 731 (White, J., concurring) (describing the "heavy burden" on the government).

55. The official gave *Jane's Fighting Ships*, a British periodical specializing in matters concerning military equipment and technology, an image taken by a U.S. satellite of a Soviet ship-building operation. The government conceded that the image itself did not harm national security but revealing the capacity and activities of U.S. satellite imagery did. U.S. v. Morison, 844 F.2d 1057 (1988). See also Bartnicki v. Vopper, 532 U.S. 514 (2001), "in which the Court held that federal and state antiwiretap statutes cannot constitutionally be applied to a radio station that broadcasts the tape of an unlawfully intercepted telephone call, where the subject of the call was a matter of public concern and the broadcaster did not participate directly in the unlawful wiretap, even though the broadcaster knew that the material had been obtained unlawfully." Stone, Constitutional Law, at 1137.

56. Nebraska Press Assoc. v. Stuart, 427 U.S. 539, 542 (1976).

57. Id. at 544 n.2.

58. Id. at 562–63.

59. Id. at 563–64, 566.

60. Id. at 573, 613.

61. Pell v. Procunier, 417 U.S. 817, 834 (1974) (internal citations omitted).

62. Id. at 840–41 (Douglas, J., dissenting).

63. See, e.g., Houchins v. KQED, Inc., 438 U.S. 1, 15–16 (1978) (holding that restrictions on access to a prison similar to the ones upheld in *Pell* are constitutional and noting that the press enjoyed the same access as the general public); Saxbe v. Washington Post Co., 417 U.S. 843, 850 (1974) (same).

64. Branzburg v. Hayes, 408 U.S. 665, 667 (1972).

65. Id. at 669–79.

66. Id. at 680.

67. Id. at 684–85.

68. Id. at 690–91.

69. Id. at 693.

70. Id. at 703.

71. Id. at 709–10 (Powell, J., concurring).

72. Id. at 725 (Stewart, J., dissenting).

73. Id. at 727–28.

74. Id. at 733.

75. Id. at 743.

76. See, e.g., Alabama Code § 12–21–142 (2008) (establishing an absolute privilege for reporters working in specified fields); California Evidence Code § 1070 (West 2009) (creating a qualified privilege in criminal cases and an absolute privilege in civil cases for both confidential and nonconfidential information); New York, McKinney's Civil Rights Law § 79-h (2008) (providing an absolute privilege for confidential information and a qualified privilege for nonconfidential information in both civil and criminal cases).

77. Free Flow of Information Act of 2009, H.R. 985, 111th Cong. (as passed by House of Representatives, Mar. 31, 2009); Free Flow of Information Act of 2009, Sen. 448, 11th Cong. (2009).

78. Richmond Newspapers, Inc. v. Virginia, 448 U.S. 555, 558 (1980).

79. Id. at 569.

80. Id. at 576 (citing *Branzburg*).

81. Id. at 587 (Brennan, J., concurring).

82. Id. at 587–88.

83. Id. at 589.

84. However, there have been several cases refining its reach. Globe Newspaper Co. v. Superior Court (1982) overturned a Massachusetts statute requiring trial judges in cases involving sexual offenses where the victim is less than eighteen to exclude the press and public from the courtroom during the testimony of the victim. 457 U.S. 596 (1982). A majority held

NOTES TO PAGES 29–34

that specific evidence for each case is needed to make a compelling case for closure. Id. at 607. Press-Enterprise Co. v. Superior Court (1984) held that voir dire hearings must be open unless specific findings meet the standard for closure. 464 U.S. 501 (1984).

85. Communications Act of 1934, ch. 652, 48 Stat. 1064 (1934) (codified as amended at 47 U.S.C. §§ 151–614, § 301 (2008)). 47 U.S.C. § 301.

86. 47 U.S.C. § 303.

87. Kay v. FCC, 443 F.2d 638, 648 (D.C. Cir. 1970).

88. Democratic Nat'l Comm. v. FCC, 481 F.2d 543, 548 (D.C. Cir. 1973).

89. The personal attack and political editorial rules refer to former 47 C.F.R. 73.1920, former 47 C.F.R. 73.1930, and former 47 C.F.R. 76.209(b), (c), and (d). These provisions were all repealed by 65 C.F.R. 6643 (2000).

90. 47 U.S.C. § 312(a)(7) (reasonable access rule), § 315(a) (equal time rule).

91. Red Lion Broad. Co. v. FCC, 395 U.S. 367, 370–73 (1969).

92. See, generally, Fred Friendly, The Good Guys, the Bad Guys and the First Amendment: Free Speech vs. Fairness in Broadcasting (1976).

93. *Red Lion*, 395 U.S. at 386.

94. Id.

95. Id. at 388–89.

96. Id. at 389.

97. Id. at 390.

98. Id. at 392.

99. Miami Herald Publ'g Co. v. Tornillo, 418 U.S. 241, 244 (1974).

100. Id. at 249–51.

101. Id. at 254.

102. Id. at 256.

103. Id. at 258.

104. See David Johnston, Court Backs F.C.C.'s Repeal of the Fairness Doctrine, N.Y. Times, Feb. 11, 1989 (reporting on D.C. Circuit upholding the FCC's repeal).

105. Voices of Reason: Thirty Years of Interviews, ReasonOnline, Dec. 1998, available at http://www.reason.com/news/show/30830.html (the interview originally appeared in "Reason Interview: Mark S. Fowler," Reason Magazine, Nov. 1, 1981).

106. Communications Act of 1934, 47 U.S.C. § 315 (2000).

107. Columbia Broad. System v. Democratic Nat'l Comm., 412 U.S. 94, 97–99 (1973).

108. FCC v. League of Women Voters, 468 U.S. 364, 366 (1984).

109. Id. at 385.

110. Id. at 385, 402.

111. See Federal Communications Commission, General Cable Television Industry and Regulation Information Fact Sheet (2000), available at http://www.fcc.gov/mb/facts/csgen.html (outlining the history of the FCC and state and local regulation of cable and discussing the requirement that FCC regulations "serve the public interest").

112. See, e.g., Geoffrey A. Berkin, Hit or Myth? The Cable TV Marketplace, Diversity and Regulation, 35 Fed. Comm. L.J. 41, 61–67 (1983) (arguing that cable is a natural monopoly); Andrew A. Bernstein, Note, Access to Cable, Natural Monopoly, and the First Amendment, 86 Colum. L. Rev. 1663 (1986) (arguing the only justification for access regulation is the cable industry's monopoly structure).

113. Turner Broad. System, Inc. v. FCC, 512 U.S. 622, 632–34 (1994).

114. Id. at 634.

115. Id. at 638–39.

116. Id. at 639–40.

117. Id. at 675.

118. Denver Area Educ. Telecomm. Consortium, Inc. v. FCC, 518 U.S. 727, 732–35 (1996).

119. FCC v. Pacifica Foundation, 438 U.S. 726 (1978).

120. Cohen v. California, 403 U.S. 15, 21–23 (1971).

121. *Denver*, 518 U.S. at 753–60.

122. U.S. v. Playboy Entertainment Group, Inc., 529 U.S. 803 (2000).

123. *Denver*, 518 U.S. at 819 (Thomas, J., concurring in part and dissenting in part).

124. 436 U.S. 775, 794 (1978).

125. Id. at 795.

126. Id. at 800.

127. Id. at 802.

128. Reno v. American Civil Liberties Union, 521 U.S. 844, 871 (1997).

129. Id. at 868–69.

130. Id. at 870.

CHAPTER 2

1. See Lee C. Bollinger, Images of a Free Press 2 (1991) (*"Sullivan* arose out of the struggle against segregation in the 1960s").

2. John Milton, Areopagitica 58 (1644; rpt., Richard C. Webb ed., 1918).

3. Abrams v. U.S., 250 U.S. 616, 630 (1919) (Holmes, J., dissenting).

4. See Lee C. Bollinger, The Tolerant Society: Freedom of Speech and Extremist Speech in America 49–50 (1986).

5. *Abrams*, 250 U.S. at 630.

6. See Bollinger, Tolerant Society, at 80–81 (noting that Alexis de Tocqueville and Mill wrote that the democratic "tyranny of the majority"

"could be every bit as threatening to basic human liberties—even more so—as the despotic political regimes that democracy had replaced").

7. 376 U.S. 254, 273 (1964).

8. See Cox v. Louisiana, 379 U.S. 536, 555 (1965) (distinguishing between "patrolling, marching, and picketing on streets and highways" and "those who communicate ideas by pure speech").

9. Nat'l Socialist Party v. Village of Skokie, 434 U.S. 1327 (1977) (marches); U.S. v. O'Brien, 391 U.S. 367 (1968) (demonstrations); Thornhill v. State of Alabama, 301 U.S. 88 (1940) (picketing); Tinker v. Des Moines Indep. Cmty. Sch. Dist., 393 U.S. 503 (1969) (armbands).

10. See O'Brien, 391 U.S. at 382–83 (finding statute was regulation of noncommunicative conduct and therefore inquiry into congressional purpose was not appropriate).

11. See Miami Herald Publ'g Co. v. Tornillo, 418 U.S. 241, 250 (1974) (finding that newspaper consolidation "place[d] in a few hands the power to inform the American people and shape public opinion").

12. Alexander Bickel, The Morality of Consent 80 (1975).

13. Id. at 87.

14. See, e.g., FCC v. Fox Television Stations, Inc., no. 07–582, 2009 WL 1118715 (U.S. Apr. 28, 2009) (Thomas, J., concurring); L. A. Powe Jr., American Broadcasting and the First Amendment (1987).

15. See, e.g., Owen M. Fiss, Why the State? 100 Harv. L. Rev. 781 (1987).

16. See Commission on Freedom of the Press, A Free and Responsible Press (1947) 14 (discussing the communications "revolution" following World War II).

17. See David Lieberman, Newsprint Costs Roll Up: Newspapers Raise Prices, Pare Stuff, USA Today, Dec. 5, 1994, at 1B (noting that the nation has 1,600 daily newspapers).

18. See, e.g., Newspaper Preservation Act, 15 U.S.C. §§ 1801–5 (2000) (first passed in 1970, this act provides for joint operating agreements to preserve editorial independence).

19. Second Report and Order, Amendment to the Rules Relating to Multiple Ownership of Standard, FM, and Television Stations, 50 F.C.C.2d 1046 (1975) (describing the cross-ownership rules).

20. See Bollinger, Images, at 28.

21. Id. at 14.

22. Id. at 15.

23. Id. at 43.

24. Id. at 31 (quoting the Hutchins Report).

25. Id. at 32 (quoting the Hutchins Report).

26. Id. at 33 (quoting the Hutchins Report).

27. See Donald R. Shanor, News from Abroad 27 (2003) (discussing Project for Excellence study).

28. Bollinger, Images, at 29 (quoting Hutchins Report).

29. See Red Lion Broad. Co. v. FCC, 395 U.S. 367, 376–77 (1969).

30. Id. at 400–401. The scarcity rationale was supplemented occasionally by one or two additional arguments for broadcast regulation. Some pointed out that broadcasting required use of the "publicly owned" spectrum, which meant the "people" had a legitimate right to regulate those to whom the public delegated the use of the space. Others openly argued that this new communication technology posed too great a risk, that it could be used to "manipulate" public opinion, which meant there had to be some government oversight. Neither of these theories worked for the purpose at hand.

31. Id. Justice Douglas recused himself in that case, but in earlier writings he had endorsed the regulation of broadcasting—because the "public owned" the airwaves.

32. Brief of American Civil Liberties Union as Amici Curiae Supporting Respondents, *Red Lion*, 395 U.S. 367 (Nos. 2 and 717).

33. Robert D. Hershey Jr., F.C.C. Votes Down Fairness Doctrine in a 4–0 Decision, N.Y. Times, Aug. 5, 1987.

34. See, generally, Ronald Coase, Evaluation of Public Policy Relating to Radio and Television Broadcasting: Social and Economic Issues, 41 Land & P.U. Econ. 161 (1965). See also Ronald Coase, The Federal Communications Commission, 2 J.L. & Econ. 1 (1959).

35. *Red Lion*, 395 U.S. at 392 ("There is no sanctuary in the First Amendment for unlimited private censorship operating in a medium not open to all. 'Freedom of the press from governmental interference under the First Amendment does not sanction repression of that freedom by private interests'").

36. See Bollinger, Images, at 94.

37. 395 U.S. 367 (1969).

38. 418 U.S. 241, 258 (1974).

CHAPTER 3

1. See Information Operations Concentration, National Defense University: Information Resources Management College (concentration for students at the National War College and the Industrial College of the Armed Forces), available at http://www.ndu.edu/IRMC/pcs_iscp.htm.

2. U.S. Military Academy, West Point, Department of Social Statistics, course catalog, available at http://www.dean.usma.edu/departments/sosh/Academic%20Program/Courses.htm.

3. Daniel Schulman, Mind Games, 45 Colum. Journalism Rev. 45, May-June 2006.

4. BBC News, U.S. Strikes at Afghan Targets, Oct. 7, 2001, available at http://news.bbc.co.uk/1/hi/world/south_asia/1556588.stm (last visited May 14, 2009).

5. Michael R. Gordon, A Nation Challenged: Public Information; Pentagon Corners Output of Special Afghan Images, N.Y. Times, Oct. 19, 2001, at B2.

6. Michael R. Gordon, A Nation Challenged: The Media; Military Is Putting Heavier Limits on Reporters' Access, N.Y. Times, Oct. 21, 2001, at B3.

7. Reporters Committee for Freedom of the Press, Pentagon Rejects Mixing Media with Ground Troops, Nov. 13, 2001, available at http://www.rcfp.org/newsitems/index.php?i=2936.

8. Carol Morello, Tight Control Marks Coverage of Afghan War; Curbs Exceed Those of the Past; Broader Access Is Promised, Wash. Post, Dec. 7, 2001, at A43.

9. David E. Rosenbaum, A Nation Challenged: The News Media; Access Limits Were an Error, Pentagon Says, N.Y. Times, Dec. 6, 2001, at B2.

10. Reporters Committee for Freedom of the Press, Press Optimistic about Improved Wartime Access, Dec. 19, 2001, available at http://www.rcfp.org/newsitems/index.php?i=2970.

11. See, e.g., Associated Press, War-Zone Reporter: Soldiers Threatened to Shoot Me, Feb. 12, 2002; Frank Rich, Freedom from the Press, N.Y. Times, Mar. 2, 2002, at A15; Reporters Committee for Freedom of the Press, Post Reporter Claims U.S. Troops Detained Him at Gunpoint (Feb. 12, 2002), available at http://www.rcfp.org/newsitems/index.php?i=3015.

12. James Dao and Eric Schmitt, A Nation Challenged: Hearts & Minds; Pentagon Readies Efforts to Sway Sentiment Abroad, N.Y. Times, Feb. 19, 2002, at A1. See also Schulman, Mind Games (including statements from interview with Brigadier General Simon P. Worden of the U.S. Air Force, who was to be named director of the OSI, on the proposed objectives and means to be used by the program).

13. See Eric Schmitt, A Nation Challenged: Hearts & Minds; A "Damaged" Information Office Is Declared Closed by Rumsfeld, N.Y. Times, Feb. 27, 2002, at A1 (noting that "[s]ince the office's proposed activities were made public...Mr. Rumsfeld repeatedly said that the Pentagon had not spread lies and that it would not do so in the future").

14. Schulman, Mind Games at 43.

15. See, e.g., James Bamford, The Man Who Sold the War, Rolling Stone, Nov. 17, 2005; Schulman, Mind Games (discussing work of John Rendon in the run-up to the invasion of Iraq and efforts to control media coverage—both foreign and domestic—of the war).

16. Schulman, Mind Games at 46 (quoting letter by General Meyers).

17. Mark Mazzetti and Borzou Daraghi, U.S. Military Covertly Pays to Run Stories in Iraqi Press, L.A. Times, Nov. 30, 2005.

18. Schulman, Mind Games.

19. Id. at 47 (quoting report).

20. For example, General Peter Pace said to the Associated Press that "[a]t the end of the day we want the United States to be seen for what it is, an open society that supports free press not only at home but overseas." Id. at 47.

21. Id. at 41 (quoting Secretary Rumsfeld).

22. Information and Educational Exchange Act of 1948, 22 U.S.C.A. § 1461 (1994). The domestic dissemination ban contained in the Smith-Mundt Act has withstood both First Amendment and Freedom of Information Act challenges. See Allen W. Palmer and Edward L. Carter, The Smith-Mundt Act's Ban on Domestic Propaganda: An Analysis of the Cold War Statute Limiting Access to Public Diplomacy, 11 Comm. L. & Pol'y 1, 15–16 (2006) (discussing three cases in which courts have dismissed challenges).

23. See USAID, Democracy & Governance Program, available at http://www.usaid.gov/our_work/democracy_and_governance (noting that one of the goals of this program is "promoting free and independent media").

24. Cf. id. (co-opting the foreign press is inapposite to the goal of promoting the development of an independent press in these countries); see also Schulman, Mind Games (discussing the report of the Free Media Working Group of the State Department's Future of Iraq Project).

25. For the AP report, see Paul G. Gardephe, Report Concerning Bilal Hussein, Associated Press Photographer–Baghdad, available at http://hosted.ap.org/specials/interactives/_documents/bh_report.pdf (last visited May 14, 2009). For coverage of the hearing, see Kim Gamel, Hearing Held for Detained AP Photographer in Iraq (Dec. 9, 2007), available at http://www.ap.org/pages/about/whatsnew/wn_120907e.html. For coverage of Hussein's release, see Robert H. Reid, AP Photographer Freed by U.S. after Two Years (Apr. 16, 2008), available at http://www.ap.org/pages/about/whatsnew/wn_041608a.html.

26. Charles Layton, Locked in Limbo, 29 Am. Journalism Rev., June–July 2007, available at http://www.ajr.org/Article.asp?id=4385 (quoting Tom Curley).

27. The Committee to Protect Journalists has reported on numerous detainees, including Majed Hameed, Fares Nawaf al-Issaywi, Samir Mohammed, and Abdul Ameer Younis Hussein. See Press Release, Committee to Protect Journalists, AP Photographer Is Latest in Long List of U.S. Detainees (Dec. 7, 2007), available at http://cpj.org/2007/12/ap-photographer-is-latest-in-long-list-of-us-detai.php.

28. News Alert, Committee to Protect Journalists, Iraqi AP Photojournalist Held by U.S. without Charge for a Year (Apr. 10, 2007), available at http://cpj.org/2007/04/iraqi-ap-photojournalist-held-by-us-without-charge.php (reporting that U.S. major general John Gardner told Reuters that the military will use a thirty-six-hour review process for all journalist detentions).

29. Kevin Rector, A Flurry of Subpoenas, 30 Am. Journalism Rev., Apr.–May 2008, available at http://www.ajr.org/Article.asp?id=4511.

30. See, e.g., Katherine Q. Seelye, Journalists Say Threat of Subpoena Intensifies, N.Y. Times, July 4, 2005, at C1 (discussing the "chillier" atmosphere for journalists seeking to protect confidential sources).

31. See Mark Jurkowitz, Pentagon, Media Debate Access Rules & Stories Keep Changing, Press Complains, Boston Globe, Mar. 20, 2002, at A26; Phillip Taylor, Pentagon "Unmuzzles" Media: Press Hesitates to Denounce War "Most Restricted" as Access Opens, News Media and the Law 11, Feb. 1, 2002, available at http://www.rcfp.org/newsitems/index.php?i=5876.

32. See, e.g., Flynt v. Rumsfeld, 355 F.3d 697 (D.C. Cir. 2004), cert. denied, 543 U.S. 925 (2004) (holding that publisher has standing, but there is no First Amendment right to "embed" journalists, and even if there were, the government restrictions are appropriate "time, place, and manner" limitations).

33. Internet World Stats, Internet Usage Statistics, https://www.internetworldstats.com/stats.htm (last visited July 5, 2009).

34. John Markoff, Internet Traffic Begins to Bypass the U.S., N.Y. Times, Aug. 30, 2008, at C1.

35. According to the Global Language Monitor, 25 percent of the world's population speaks English. English Spoken Here, as It Is Everywhere, Kansas City (Mo.) Star, Aug. 19, 2008, at B9.

36. UN Conference on Trade and Development, FDI Stats Online, available at http://stats.unctad.org/FDI.

37. The United States, France, Germany, and Japan are all OECD members. For a complete list of OECD member countries, see Ratification of the Convention on the OECD, available at http://www.oecd.org/docum ent/58/0,3343,en_2649_201185_1889402_1_1_1_1,00.html.

38. James D. Wolfensohn, This Summit's Promise, Wash. Post, Nov. 14, 2008, at A19.

39. UN World Tourism Organization, Tourism Highlights 1 (2008), available at http://www.unwto.org/facts/eng/pdf/highlights/UNWTO_Highlights08_en_LR.pdf.

40. UN World Tourism Organization, Tourism 2020 Vision, available at http://www.unwto.org/facts/eng/vision.htm (last visited May 14, 2009).

41. Press Release, Institute of International Education, U.S. Study Abroad Up 8%, Continuing Decade-Long Growth (Nov. 17, 2008), available at http://opendoors.iienetwork.org/?p=131592.

42. Id. Though students are increasingly studying internationally, the number of American citizens as a whole traveling outside the country every year has remained steady, at about 20 percent. U.S. Census Bureau, 2009 Statistical Abstract, available at http://www.census.gov/compendia/statab/cats/arts_recreation_travel.html.

43. Vince Stricherz, Dust Particles from Asian Deserts Common over Western United States, Univ. of Wash. News, Dec. 13, 2007, available at http://uwnews.org/article.asp?articleid=38562.

44. See David A. Taylor, Dust in the Wind, 110 Envtl. Health Persp. A84 (2002) (noting that bacteria and fungi that attach to dust clouds "may be related to recent increases in asthma rates"); Mark Grossi, Ozone Levels Drop along with Temperatures, Fresno Bee, Aug. 20, 2008, at B1 (noting California's increased asthma rate); Barbara Feder

Ostrov, Asthma Afflicts 12% in State, Study Says, San Jose Mercury News, May 7, 2002, at A1 (noting that an estimated 12 percent of the population, 3.9 million people, have been diagnosed with asthma at some point in their lives).

45. Daily weekday circulation as of 2008 was as follows: *Wall Street Journal*, 2 million; *New York Times*, 1 million; *Los Angeles Times*, 739,000; *Washington Post*, 683,000. Richard Perez-Pena, Newspaper Circulation Continues to Decline Rapidly, N.Y. Times, Oct. 28, 2008, at B4; Profits Drop 39% at Washington Post Company, N.Y. Times, May 3, 2008, at C2.

46. Doreen Carvajal, The Times and I.H.T. Study Web Merger, N.Y. Times, June 24, 2008, at C2.

47. See, e.g., Mark Trumbull, The Tribune Company's Bankruptcy May Signal a Trend toward a New Kind of Newspaper, Christian Sci. Monitor, Dec. 10, 2008, at 2 ("For newspapers, advertising revenues have been falling since 2006, and the most recent quarter [shows] a record percentage decline of 18 percent"); Web, Not Bias, Offing Papers, Denver Rocky Mountain News, Dec. 13, 2008, at 24 ("Subscription declines are very bad long-term for newspapers, but the more immediate, and perhaps fatal problem is the decline in advertising revenues"); Katherine Yung, Publishing Decision Is Bold, But Not Without Risks, Detroit Free Press, Dec. 17, 2008 (noting that "newspapers have been battling dramatic decline[s] in circulation and advertising revenues").

48. Although the *Wall Street Journal* has more than 650,000 online subscribers, the *New York Times* tried to required subscriptions to access online content "but found there was too much free competition." See Shanor, News from Abroad, at 190.

49. Rupert Murdoch of News Corp. on the Future of Newspapers, Facebook vs. MySpace and Why He Didn't Sue YouTube, Wall St. J., June 9, 2008, at R6.

50. Lorraine Mirabella, Sun, Hurt by Revenue Declines, to Eliminate 100 Jobs, Balt. Sun, June 26, 2008 (discussing how many newspapers are cutting staff).

51. Richard Perez-Pena, Papers Facing Worst Year for Ad Revenue, N.Y. Times, June 23, 2008, at C3.

52. Shira Ovide, Philadelphia Inquirer Publisher Files for Chapter 11, Wall. St. J., Feb. 23, 2009, available at http://online.wsj.com/article/SB123536209736046065.html.

53. Richard Perez-Pena, Times Co. Posts a Loss of $74.5 Million, N.Y. Times, Apr. 22, 2009, at B6.

54. Tim Arango, CBS Is Said to Consider Use of CNN in Reporting, N.Y. Times, Apr. 8, 2008, at C1.

55. Richard Perez-Pena, L.A. Times Newsroom to Shrink by 150 Jobs, N.Y. Times, July 3, 2008, at C3.

56. Jenna Wortham, News about News, in 140 Characters, N.Y. Times, Dec. 15, 2008, at B4.

57. Shanor, News from Abroad, at 7.

58. Paul Starr, Goodbye to the Age of Newspapers (Hello to a New Era of Corruption), New Republic, Mar. 4, 2009, available at http://www.tnr.com/politics/story.html?id=a4e2aafc-cc92–4e79–90d1-db3946a6d119.

59. William A. Hachten, The Troubles of Journalism 17 (2005). Indeed, "[a]s U.S. news organizations have backed away from foreign news coverage, the Associated Press' international report has become increasingly vital." Sherry Ricchiardi, Covering the World, 29 Am. Journalism Rev., Dec. 2007–Jan. 2008, at 32.

60. Ernesto Londoño and Amit R. Paley, Western Journalists in Iraq Stage Pullback of Their Own, Wash. Post, Nov. 10, 2008, at A1; Seth Mnookin, The New York Times's Lonely War, Vanity Fair, Dec. 2008.

61. Richard Perez-Pena, As Papers Struggle, News Is Cut and the Focus Turns Local, N.Y. Times, July 21, 2008, at C6.

62. Survey Reports, Pew Research Centre for the People and the Press, Key News Audiences Now Blend Online and Traditional Sources, Aug. 17, 2008, available at http://people-press.org/report/?pageid=1356.

63. Shanor, News from Abroad, at 189.

64. Id. at 36.

65. Id. at 189.

66. Press Release, National Public Radio, NPR Reaches New Audience High as Listeners Seek In-Depth News on Election, Economy, Mar. 24, 2009, available at http://www.npr.org/about/press/2009/032409.Audience Record.html.

67. Associated Press, Facts and Figures (Apr. 16, 2007), available at http://www.ap.org/pages/about/about.html.

68. Jay Newton-Small, The AP Is Breaking More than News, Wash. Post, Oct. 25, 2008.

69. See Press Release, Associated Press, The Associated Press Teams with MSN to Launch the AP Online Video Network (Mar. 1, 2006) ("The Associated Press is the world's oldest and largest newsgathering organization, providing content to more than 15,000 news outlets with a daily reach of 1 billion people").

70. Ethan Bronner, Israel Puts Media Clamp on Gaza, N.Y. Times, Jan. 6, 2009, at A2.

71. Ropy Alampay, No News Is Bad News, N.Y. Times, May 5, 2008, at A19 ("All broadcast systems are state-owned and the largest newspapers are controlled by the government"); Jonathan Head, UN Warning over Burma Cyclone Aid, BBC News, May 2, 2009, available at http://news.bbc.co.uk/2/hi/asia-pacific/8030211.stm (noting that foreign journalists are banned from reporting in Burma).

72. Celia W. Duggar, Mbeki Visits Zimbabwe as Violence Worsens, N.Y. Times, May 10, 2008, at A9.

73. Salman Masood, In Pakistan, Bill to Lift Restrictions on the Media, N.Y. Times, Apr. 12, 2008, at A8.

74. See Committee to Protect Journalists, At Least 13 Jailed as Crackdown Enters Second Week, June 22, 2009, available at http://cpj.org/2009/06/in-iran-massive-media-crackdown-enters-second-week.php; Najmeh Bozorgmehr, Twitter Goes On But Foreign TV Takes Lead Role, Fin. Times, June 18, 2009, available at http://www.ft.com/cms/s/0/4c7dcdf2-5b9e-11de-be3f-00144feabdc0.html; Nazila Fathi, Protesters Defy Iranian Efforts to Cloak Unrest, N.Y. Times, June 18, 2009, at A1; Brian Stelter, Real Time Criticism of CNN's Iran Coverage, N.Y. Times, June 15, 2009, at B5.

75. Edward Cody, For China's Journalism Students, Censorship Is a Core Concept, Wash. Post, Dec. 31, 2007, at A11.

76. Press Release, Committee to Protect Journalists, China Must Address Press Freedom in Tibet, Mar. 9, 2009, available at http://cpj.org/2009/03/china-must-address-press-freedom-in-tibet.php.

77. See, e.g., Jane Macartney, Time Out Magazine Banned by China's Censors in Run Up to Olympics, TimesOnline (U.K.), June 11, 2008, available at http://www.timesonline.co.uk/tol/news/world/asia/article4113093.ece (discussing difficulties faced by American magazines in China).

78. Canadian Radio-Television and Telecommunications Commission, Mandate, available at http://www.crtc.gc.ca/eng/cancon/mandate.htm (last updated Nov. 1, 2007).

76. European Commission, Audiovisual Media Services Directive, available at http://ec.europa.eu/avpolicy/reg/avms/index_en.htm (last visited May 14, 2009).

80. See Mira Burri-Nenova, Trade and Culture: Making the WTO Legal Framework Conducive to Cultural Considerations 19–20 (NCCR Trade Regulation, Working Paper 2008/20), available at http://papers.ssrn.com/sol3/papers.cfm?abstract_id=1306911.

81. James Lamont, India Relaxes Restrictions on Foreign Media, Fin. Times, Sept. 20, 2008, at 7.

82. Id.

83. See Mark Landler and Brian Stelter, With a Hint to Twitter, Washington Taps Into a Potent New Force in Diplomacy, N.Y. Times, June 17, 2009, at A12; Brad Stone and Noam Cohen, Social Networks Spread Iranian Defiance Online, N.Y. Times, June 16, 2009, at A11; Charley Keyes, Iranian-Americans "Hungry" For Updates Amid Tumult in Iran, CNN.com, June 17, 2009, at http://www.google.com/search?q=iranian+americans+hungry+for+news+from+iran+amid+tumult&sourceid=navclient-ff&ie=UTF-8&rlz=1B3DVFC_en___US319.

84. Council on Foreign Relations, Media Censorship in China (Mar. 18, 2008), available at http://www.cfr.org/publication/11515.

85. Janine Zacharia, Google, Web Access and Censorship, Bloomberg News, June 3, 2008.

86. See Tom Krazit, Google's Censorship Struggles Continue in China, CNet, June 16, 2009, available at http://news.cnet.com/8301–17939 109–10265123–2.html; Edward Wong, China Disables Some Google Functions, N.Y. Times, June 19, 2009, available at http://www.nytimes.com/ 2009/06/20/world/asia/20beijing.html; Edward Wong, China Orders Patches to Planned Web Filter, N.Y. Times, June 15, 2009, at http://www. nytimes.com/2009/06/16/business/global/16censor.html.

87. Michael Wines and Andrew Jacobs, To Shut Off Tiananmen Talk, China Blocks More Web Sites, N.Y. Times, June 3, 2009, at A13.

88. United Kingdom Representation in China, House of Commons, Select Committee on Foreign Affairs, Tenth Report, Nov. 29, 2000, available at http://www.publications.parliament.uk/pa/cm199900/cmselect/ cmfaff/574/57412.htm.

89. Memorandum from the BBC on its experience of the suppression of human rights–related reporting to House of Commons, Select Committee on Foreign Affairs (May 1998), available at http://www.publications.parliament.uk/pa/cm199899/cmselect/cmfaff/100/8051206.htm.

90. Martin Wolf, Why Putin's Rule Threatens Both Russia and the West, Fin. Times, Feb. 12, 2008, at 9.

91. Committee to Protect Journalists, Journalist, Human Rights Lawyer Shot Dead in Moscow, Jan. 20, 2009, available at http://cpj.org/2009/01/ journalist-and-human-rights-lawyer-shot-dead-in-mo.php; Andrew Osborn, Kremlin's Concern for Journalist Draws Skepticism from Critics, Wall St. J., Dec. 3, 2008, at A10. See also Editorial, More Moscow Murder: Two Critics of Vladimir Putin Take Bullets in the Head, Wash. Post, Jan. 20, 2009, at A24 (stating that it is "indisputable...that Russians live in a political climate in which those who criticize Mr. Putin or the human rights violations of his government can be murdered with impunity").

92. See Michael Schwirtz, Leading Russian Rights Lawyer Shot to Death in Moscow along with a Journalist, N.Y. Times, Jan. 20, 2009, at A6.

93. Andrew Higgins, Why Islam Is Unfunny for a Cartoonist, Wall St. J., July 12, 2008, at W1.

94. Christopher Caldwell, In Defence of the Right to Offend, Fin. Times, Jan. 26, 2008.

95. See Editorial, Honoring Rushdie, N.Y. Times, June 26, 2007, at A20 (noting that Rushdie's knighthood raises the question: "Do we choose to live in a world that honors writers or in a world that kills them?").

96. Monica Campbell and María Salazar, Committee to Protect Journalists, The Disappeared in Mexico (Sept. 2008), available at http://cpj.org/reports/2008/09/mexico-08.php.

97. Yigal Schleifer, Turkey Tightens Control on Internet Speech, Christian Sci. Monitor, Oct. 30, 2008, at 6.

98. Seth Mydans and Mark McDonald, Novelist Given 3 Years for Insulting Thai King, N.Y. Times, Jan. 20, 2009, at A8 (quoting a source as saying, "Thailand is trying to send a message to international media, to writers, to bloggers, to people who are putting material on the Internet, that the royal family is out of bounds").

99. Libel Reform: Freer Speech, Economist, Mar. 2, 1996, at 55; Duncan Campbell, British Libel Laws Violate Human Rights, Says U.N., Guardian (U.K.), Aug. 14, 2008.

100. Warren Hoge, Intervention, Hailed as a Concept, Is Shunned in Practice, N.Y. Times, Jan. 20, 2008, at A12.

101. S.C. Res. 1674, UN Doc. S/RES/1674 (Apr. 28, 2006).

102. Jeffrey Rosen, Google's Gatekeepers, N.Y. Times Magazine, Nov. 28, 2008, at 50; Italy Is to File Charges against Google Executives, Wall St. J., July 25, 2008, at B7.

103. Sheikh It All About, Economist, Nov. 10, 2007, at 73–74.

104. Sarah Lyall, Are Saudis Using British Libel Law to Deter Critics? N.Y. Times, May 22, 2004, at B7.

105. James Oliphant, Saudi Wields British Law against U.S. Author: Billionaire Leverages Harsher Libel Rules to Suppress Unflattering Book, Chi. Trib., Mar. 17, 2008, at C4.

106. Press Release, New York State, Governor Paterson Signs Legislation Protecting New Yorkers against Infringement of First Amendment Rights by Foreign Libel Judgments (May 1, 2008), available at http://www.state. ny.us/governor/press/press_0501082.html.

107. Arlen Specter and Joe Lieberman, Foreign Courts Take Aim at Our Free Speech, Wall St. J., July 14, 2008, at A15.

108. Floyd Abrams, Foreign Law and the First Amendment, Wall St. J., Apr. 30, 2008, at A15.

109. Newsweek Media Kit, Newsweek Europe Edition: Fuel for Active Minds, available at http://www.thinknewsweek.com/index.html (last visited July 6, 2009); Time Media Kit, 2008 Time EMEA Circulation, available at http://www.time.com/time/mediakit/1/emea/timemagazine/circulation/index.html (last visited May 14, 2009).

110. RSS Content, New York Times Company, International Herald Tribune Joins Forces with the New York Times on the Web and Reveals New Look, Mar. 30, 2009, available at http://phx.corporate-ir.net/phoenix. zhtml?c=105317&p=RssLanding&cat=news&id=1271003.

111. CCTV, About CCTV International, at http://www.cctv.com/english/ about/index.shtml; CCTV, CCTV Launches Arabic International Channel, July 26, 2009, at http://www.cctv.com/program/worldwidewatch/20090726/ 101399.shtml.

112. Al Jazeera TV Viewer Demographic, Allied Media Corp, available at http://www.allied-media.com/aljazeera/JAZdemog.html (last visited May 15, 2009).

113. How to Watch Al Jazeera, AlJazeera.net, available at http://english. aljazeera.net/watchaje/2008717114526698333.html (last visited May 15, 2009).

114. Economist, World Circulation, July–Dec. 2008, available at http://ads. economist.com/the-economist/circulation/worldwide-circulation.

115. Leslie Crawford, Prisa Sets Sights on U.S. Conquest, Fin. Times, Feb. 26, 2008, at 22.

116. BBC, About the BBC, available at http://www.bbc.co.uk/info/purpose (last visited May 15, 2009).

117. BBC, History of the BBC, available at http://www.bbc.co.uk/heritage/story/index.shtml (last visited May 15, 2009).

118. British Broadcasting Corporation, BBC Response to a Strong BBC: Independent of Government 3 (May 2005), available at http://www.bbc.co.uk/info/policies/pdf/green_paper_response.pdf.

119. BBC Press Office, BBC Trust Members, available at http://www.bbc.co.uk/bbctrust/about/bbc_trust_members/index.html (last visited May 15, 2009).

120. BBC, Royal Charter (July 19, 2006), available at http://www.bbc.co.uk/bbctrust/assets/files/pdf/regulatory_framework/charter_agreement/royalchartersealed_septo6.pdf.

121. BBC Press Office, The TV Licence Fee, available at http://www.bbc.co.uk/pressoffice/keyfacts/stories/licencefee.shtml (last visited May 15, 2009); BBC, Annual Report and Accounts 2007/08, at 105 (June 19, 2008), available at http://downloads.bbc.co.uk/annualreport/pdf/bbc_ara_2008_exec.pdf.

122. Id.

123. U.K. Department for Culture, Media, and Sport, An Agreement between Her Majesty's Secretary of State for Culture, Media and Sport and the British Broadcasting Corporation (July 2006), available at http://www.bbc.co.uk/bbctrust/assets/files/pdf/regulatory_framework/charter_agreement/bbcagreement_july06.txt.

124. BBC, About the BBC (Jan. 24, 2009), available at http://www.bbc.co.uk/info/purpose/what.shtml; Press Release, British Broadcasting Corporation, World Service Receives £70 Million Funding Increase over Next Three Years in Comprehensive Spending Review (Oct. 9, 2007), available at http://www.bbc.co.uk/pressoffice/pressreleases/stories/2007/10_october/09/ws.shtml.

125. Press Release, British Broadcasting Corporation, BBC World Service Announces "Biggest Transformation in 70 Years" (Oct. 25, 2005), available at http://www.bbc.co.uk/pressoffice/pressreleases/stories/2005/10_october/25/world.shtml.

126. BBC, World Service Receives £70 Million Funding Increase.

127. John F. Burns, Persian Station in Britain Rattles Officials in Iran, N.Y. Times, June 29, 2009, at A8.

128. BBC, BBC Response to a Strong BBC.

129. Shanor, News from Abroad, at 15.

130. Broadcasting Board of Governors, Fiscal Year 2008 Budget Request: Executive Summary 8, available at http://www.bbg.gov/reports/budget/ bbg_fy08_budget_request.pdf; see also Broadcasting Board of Governors, BBG Fast Facts, available at http://www.bbg.gov/office/index.html (last visited May 15, 2009); Radio Free Europe/Radio Liberty, About RFE/RL, available at http://www.rferl.org/info/history/133.html (last updated Dec. 2008).

131. Voice of America, About VOA, available at http://www.voanews.com/ english/about/VOAHistory.cfm (last visited May 15, 2009).

132. Voice of America, VOA Charter, available at http://www.voanews. com/english/about/VOACharter.cfm (last visited May 15, 2009).

133. Radio Free Europe/Radio Liberty, About RFE/RL: Mission Statement, available at http://www.rferl.org/info/about/176.html (last visited May 15, 2009).

134. U.S.–Funded Arab Language TV Network under Scrutiny (PBS *NewsHour* television broadcast, June 23, 2008).

135. U.S.–Funded Arab TV's Credibility Crisis (CBS *60 Minutes* television broadcast, June 22, 2008).

136. Al Hurra Missteps Echo Other U.S.–Backed Media (NPR *All Things Considered* radio broadcast, June 24, 2008).

137. U.S.–Funded Arab Language TV Network under Scrutiny.

138. Information and Educational Exchange Act of 1948, 22 U.S.C.A. § 1461 (1994).

139. International Broadcasting Act of 1994, Title III § 304, Pub. L. no. 103–236, 108 Stat. 434 (codified as amended at 22 U.S.C. § 6203 (2008)).

140. U.S.–Funded Arab TV's Credibility Crisis.

141. U.S. Broadcasting Reorganization Act of 2008, H.R. 7070, 110th Cong. (2008).

CHAPTER 4

1. Pulitzer Prize, Entry Form, Q&A, available at http://www.pulitzer.org/files/entryforms/Bulletin%20Q&A-FINAL.pdf (last visited May 14, 2009).

2. UN General Assembly, Resolution 59(I), Dec. 14, 1946, available at http://daccessdds.un.org/doc/RESOLUTION/GEN/NR0/033/10/IMG/NR003310.pdf?OpenElement. The UN General Assembly noted, "Freedom of information is a fundamental human right and is the touch-stone of all the freedoms to which the United Nations is consecrated."

3. Paul Collier, The Bottom Billion: Why the Poorest Countries Are Failing and What Can Be Done about It 3, 99–123 (2007).

4. Id. at 38–52.

5. Id. at 17–35.

6. Id. at 147–48.

7. Nathan Sachs, "Freedom of the Press, Democracy & Democratization" Paper presented at the annual meeting of the Midwest Political Science Association, Chicago, April 2007.

8. Madeleine K. Albright and William S. Cohen, Preventing Genocide: A Blueprint for U.S. Policymakers 49 (2008), available at http://www.usip.org/genocide_taskforce/report.html:

> Free and responsible media are critical to ensuring that both citizens and governing elites are well informed and that citizens are able to hold their government accountable. Independence from state control and a multiplicity of independent outlets are essential not only for the integrity of information, but also [for] promoting healthy political dialogue and supporting language

and cultural preferences. It is also important that the media develop a sense of ethical responsibility, supporting the rule of law and diminishing intergroup tensions.

9. See New York Passes Law against "Libel Tourists," Times Online (U.K.), Feb. 29, 2008 (discussing enactment of the Libel Terrorism Protection Act in New York), available at http://business.timesonline.co.uk/tol/business/law/article3461623.ece; Peter Hannaford, Tourist Trap, Am. Spectator, Apr. 13, 2009, available at http://spectator.org/archives/2009/04/13/the-worst-kind-of-tourist (discussing enactment of Illinois law). See also Rachel Ehrenfeld, California Acts to Stop Libel Tourism, Huffington Post, May 5, 2009, available at http://www.huffingtonpost.com/dr-rachel-ehrenfeld/california-acts-to-stop-l_b_196666.html (urging California legislature to pass proposed anti–libel tourism act).

10. Universal Declaration of Human Rights, G.A. Res. 217A, UN GAOR, 3d sess., 1st plen. mtg., UN Doc. A/810 (Dec. 12, 1948).

11. Alexander M. Bickel, The Morality of Consent 80 (1977) (noting that the outcome of the *Pentagon Papers Case* resulted in "a disorderly situation surely").

12. See Hague v. CIO, 307 U.S. 496 (1939).

13. Id. at 515.

14. See, e.g., U.S. v. Kokinda, 497 U.S. 720, 730 (1990) (holding that a sidewalk entirely on post office property is not a public forum); International Society for Krishna Consciousness v. Lee, 505 U.S. 672, 680 (1992) (holding that an airport terminal is not a public forum).

15. See Richmond Newspapers, Inc. v. Virginia, 448 U.S. 555, 573 (1980) (noting that "media representatives enjoy the same right of access [to a criminal trial] as the public").

16. See id. at 576 ("[W]e have recognized that 'without some protection for seeking out the news, freedom of the press could be eviscerated'" [quoting Branzburg v. Hayes, 408 U.S. 665, 681 (1972)]).

17. See, e.g., Ben Fox, Military Blocks Media Access to Guantanamo, Wash. Post, June 15, 2006 (reporting that, after allowing over 1,000 journalists

to visit the Guantanamo Bay military base since the U.S. military began using the facility to detain "suspected al-Qaida [*sic*] and Taliban militants… the Pentagon has shut down access entirely—at least temporarily").

18. 403 U.S. 15, 22–23 (1971).

19. FCC v. Fox Television Stations, Inc., no. 07–582, 2009 WL 1118715 (U.S. Apr. 28, 2009) (deciding the case on nonconstitutional grounds).

20. FCC v. Pacifica Foundation, 438 U.S. 726, 731 n.2 (1978).

21. See Cohen v. California, 403 U.S. 15, 21 (1971) ("Those in the Los Angeles courthouse could effectively avoid further bombardment of their sensibilities simply by averting their eyes").

22. See Letter from William P. Tayman Jr., Corp. for Pub. Broad. to Board of Directors, Corp. for Pub. Broad. (Sept. 23, 2008), available at http://www.cpb.org/aboutcpb/leadership/board/resolutions/080923_fy09-OperatingBudget.pdf (noting proposed federal appropriation for fiscal year 2009 is $400 million combined for television and radio).

23. See Public Broadcasting Service, About PBS: Corporate Facts, available at http://www.pbs.org/aboutpbs/aboutpbs_corp.html (last visited May 14, 2009) (reporting "168 noncommercial, educational licensees operat[ing] 356 PBS member stations"); National Public Radio, About NPR, available at http://www.npr.org/about (last visited May 14, 2009) ("NPR serves a growing audience of 26 million Americans each week in partnership with more than 860 independently operated, noncommercial public radio stations").

24. See Diversity for the Radio Waves, L.A. Times, Sept. 13, 1999, at 4 (noting that, in 1996, the FCC gave $70 billion worth of digital spectrum licenses to commercial broadcasters).

25. 47 U.S.C. § 534(b)(1)(A).

26. See Press Release, New York Times Co., The New York Times Chooses Transcontinental to Expand Its Presence in Toronto (Nov. 28, 2005), available at http://phx.corporate-ir.net/phoenix.zhtml?c=105317&p=irol-pressArticle&ID=790459&highlight= ("We are continuing to execute against our plan to increase circulation of our national edition").

27. BBC Press Office, The TV Licence Fee, available at http://www.bbc. co.uk/pressoffice/keyfacts/stories/licencefee.shtml (last updated Apr. 2009); BBC, Annual Report and Accounts 2007/08 105 (June 19, 2008), available at http://downloads.bbc.co.uk/annualreport/pdf/bbc_ara_2008_exec.pdf.

28. See Letter from William P. Tayman Jr., Corp. for Pub. Broad.

29. David Stone, *Nixon and the Politics of Public Television*, 288–301.

30. FCC v. League of Women Voters, 468 U.S. 364, 396–99 (1984).

31. See Wilson P. Dizard, Inventing Public Diplomacy: The Story of the U.S. Information Agency 142 (2004) (noting that Radio Free Europe was created partly as a response to criticisms that the Voice of America was not aggressive enough at attacking the Soviet Union, even though the VOA had shifted from its "full and fair" mandate to directly attacking the Soviet Union).

32. See Hugh Miles, Al-Jazeera 375 (2005) ("Al-Hurrah was just the Voice of America under a different name").

33. UN General Assembly, Resolution 59(I), Dec. 14, 1946, available at http://daccessdds.un.org/doc/RESOLUTION/GEN/NR0/033/10/IMG/ NR003310.pdf?OpenElement. The International Covenant on Civil and Political Rights was passed in 1966 and the Universal Declaration of Human Rights in 1948.

34. Mary Ann Glendon, A World Made New: Eleanor Roosevelt and the Universal Declaration of Human Rights 53–72 (2001).

35. See Louis Henkin et al., Human Rights 147 (2d ed. 2009) (noting that the UDHR was "seen as but a 'second best'" to a "legally binding Bill of Rights").

36. See, e.g., Mark W. Janis, An Introduction to International Law 259–60 (4th ed. 2003); Geraldine Van Bueren, The International Law on the Rights of the Child 18 (1995); Shayna Kadidal, "Federalizing" Immigration Law: International Law as a Limitation on Congress's Power to Legislate in the Field of Immigration, 77 Fordham L. Rev. 501, 516 (2008).

37. See Louis Henkin, The Age of Rights 6–10 (1990).

38. Universal Declaration of Human Rights, art. 19, G.A. Res. 217A, at 71, UN GAOR, 3d sess., 1st plen. mtg., UN Doc. A/810 (Dec. 12, 1948).

39. Compare International Covenant on Civil and Political Rights, art. 19, opened for signature Dec. 19, 1966, 999 U.N.T.S. 171, with Organization of American States, American Convention on Human Rights, art. 13, Nov. 22, 1969, O.A.S.T.S. no. 36, 1144 U.N.T.S. 123, available at http://www.oas.org/juridico/english /treaties/b-32.html; European Convention for the Protection of Human Rights and Fundamental Freedoms, art. 10, Nov. 4, 1950, 213 U.N.T.S. 222. Article 9 of the African [Banjul] Charter on Human and People's Rights includes a sparser provision: "Every individual [shall] have the right to receive information" and "[e]very individual shall have the right to express and disseminate his opinions within the law." OAU Doc. CAB/LEG/67/3, rev. 5, 21 ILM 58 (Oct. 21, 1986).

40. See, e.g., Report of the Special Rapporteur, Promotion and Protection of the Right to Freedom of Opinion and Expression, UN Doc. E/CN.4/1998/40, Jan. 28, 1998, para. 14 (arguing that "the right to seek, receive and impart information imposes a positive obligation on States to ensure access to information, particularly with regard to information held by Government in all types of storage and retrieval systems").

41. Ballantyne and Davidson v. Canada, communication no. 359/1989, and McIntyre v. Canada, communication no. 385/1989, UN Docs. CCPR/C/47/D/359/1989 and 385/1989/Rev. 1, May 5, 1993, annex, para. 11.3.

42. This presumption is contained in Article 2 of the International Covenant on Civil and Political Rights itself, which notes that the obligations of signatory states extend only to those individuals "within its territory and subject to its jurisdiction." International Covenant on Civil and Political Rights.

43. Human Rights Committee, General Comment 10: Freedom of Expression, art. 19, 19th sess., 1983, available at http://www.unhchr.ch/tbs/doc.nsf/(Symbol)/2bb2f14bf558182ac12563ed0048df17?Opendocument.

44. See UN Treaty Collection, Status of the International Covenant on Civil and Political Rights, http://treaties.un.org/Pages/ViewDetails.aspx?src=TREATY&mtdsg_no=IV-4&chapter=4&lang=en (last visited May 15, 2009). It is important to remember that many of these states have

submitted reservations and declarations limiting the force of the treaty as it applies to these countries.

45. There is a third enforcement mechanism—state communications—but it has never been used. Henkin et al., Human Rights, at 455.

46. Id.

47. See id. at 453–54 (discussing benefits of "shadow reports").

48. Report of the Human Rights Committee, vol. 1, UN Doc. A/61/40, at 18–19 (2006) (including a table of overdue reports).

49. Of the 164 states that are a party to the ICCPR, 111 have also ratified the Optional Protocol. See UN Treaty Collection, Status of the Optional Protocol to the International Covenant on Civil and Political Rights, available at http://treaties.un.org/Pages/ViewDetails.aspx?src=TREATY& mtdsg_no=IV-5&chapter=4&lang=en (last visited May 15, 2009) (listing states that have ratified or signed the Optional Protocol in real time).

50. Laurence R. Helfer and Anne-Marie Slaughter, Toward a Theory of Effective Supranational Adjudication, 107 Yale L.J. 273, 343, 349–51 (1997).

51. Henkin et al., Human Rights, at 455.

52. See, e.g., Bleier v. Uruguay, Hum. Rts. Comm., 1982, UN Doc. A/37/40, at 130 (1982) (finding that the "State party has ignored the Committee's repeated requests for a thorough inquiry into the authors' allegations" of disappearance and proceeding based on the facts provided by the complainant).

53. Helfer and Slaughter, Toward a Theory, at 344–45.

54. Id. at 345 (referring to Follow-Up Activities under the Optional Protocol, UN GAOR, Hum. Rts. Comm., 50th sess., supp. no. 40, at 96, UN Doc. A/50/40 (1995)).

55. Report of the Human Rights Committee, at 2, 108–29 (noting the lack of compliance and providing a comprehensive survey of individual state's actions).

56. For praise of the European Court, see Helfer and Slaughter, Toward a Theory, at 296 and n. 96. A study by Professors Darren Hawkins and Wade Jacoby found that compliance (to a certain degree of "satisfaction") with

Inter-American Court decisions may be as high as 76 percent. Partial Compliance: A Comparison of the European and Inter-American Courts for Human Rights 4 (Aug. 18, 2009) (unpublished manuscript), available at http://www.allacademic.com//meta/p_mla_apa_research_citation/2/7/8/9/3/pages278931/p278931–1.php.

57. See World Trade Organization, Members and Observers, available at http://www.wto.org/english/theWTO_e/whatis_e/tif_e/org6_e.htm (last updated July 23, 2008) (listing member countries and dates of membership).

58. See Sarah Cleveland, Norm Internationalization and U.S. Economic Sanctions, 26 Yale J. Int'l L. 1, 66 (2001) ("Although the recent WTO talks in Seattle brought unprecedented attention to the relationship between WTO trade issues and labor, environmental, and other social concerns, the talks failed to make any progress toward accommodating these considerations in the free trade principles of the GATT").

59. Bruno De Witte, Trade in Culture: International Legal Regimes and EU Constitutional Values, *in* The EU and the WTO: Legal and Constitutional Issues 237–38 (Grainne De Burca and Joanne Scott eds., 2001).

60. General Agreement on Tariffs and Trade, Oct. 30, 1947, 61 Stat. A-11, 55 U.N.T.S. 194.

61. See De Witte, Trade in Culture, at 242 (analyzing the cultural exceptions placed in the original text of the GATT).

62. Mira Burri-Nenova, Trade and Culture: Making the WTO Legal Framework Conducive to Cultural Considerations 17 (NCCR Trade Regulation, Working Paper no. 2008/20), 2008, available at http://papers.ssrn.com/sol3/papers.cfm?abstract_id=1306911.

63. See World Trade Organization, Understanding the WTO: Basics, available at http://www.wto.org/english/theWTO_e/whatis_e/tif_e/fact2_e.htm (last visited May 14, 2009).

64. Kim Sung-jin, Korea to Halve Screen Quota, Korea Times, Jan. 27, 2006.

65. Tim Wu, The World Trade Law of Internet Filtering (May 3, 2006), available at http://papers.ssrn.com/sol3/papers.cfm?abstract_id=882459.

66. See Appellate Body Report, Canada: Certain Measures Concerning Periodicals, WT/DS31/AB/R (June 30, 1997).

67. International Centre for Trade and Sustainable Development, EU, U.S. Initiate[s] WTO Dispute Proceedings against Chinese News Regulations, 12 Bridges Wkly. Trade News Digest, Feb. 20, 2008, available at http://ictsd.net/i/news/bridgesweekly/11085.

68. Id.

69. International Centre for Trade and Sustainable Development, China to Ease Restrictions on Foreign News Providers, 12 Bridges Wkly. Trade News Digest, Nov. 19, 2008, available at http://ictsd.net/i/news/bridgesweekly/33956.

70. First Submission of the United States, China—Measures Affecting Trading Rights and Distribution Services for Certain Publications and Audiovisual Entertainment Products, WT/DS363/5, ¶¶ 4, 48 (May 13, 2008).

71. Bradley S. Klapper, US Wins Major Trade Victory Over China, Associated Press, Aug. 12, 2009, available at http://www.time.com/time/world/article/0,8599,1915938,00.html; World Trade Organization, Dispute Settlement: Dispute DS363, available at http://www.wto.org/english/tratop_e/dispu_e/cases_e/ds362_e.htm (last updated Jan. 21, 2009).

72. Michael Wines, China Scales Back Software Filter Plan, N.Y. Times, Aug. 13, 2009. See Keith Bradsher, Beijing Adds Curbs On Access to Internet, N.Y. Times, June 26, 2009, at A4; Loretta Chao, Big Business Groups Complain to China's Premier, Wall St. J., June 27–28, 2009, at A6; Kim Hart, U.S. Presses China on Censorship, Wash. Post., June 25, 2009, at A14; Editorial, Internet Censorship, Fin. Times, June 29, 2009. See also Loretta Chao and Jason Dean, Chinese Delay Plan For Censor Software, Wall St. J., July 1, 2009, at A1 (reporting Chinese government's decision to indefinitely delay implementation of the filter rule).

73. See UN Conference on Trade and Development, Recent Developments in International Investment Agreements 2 (2008), available at http://www.unctad.org/en/docs/webdiaeia2008L_en.pdf (counting 2,608 BITs at the end of 2007). See also America's Trade Compliance Center, available at

http://tcc.export.gov/Trade_Agreements/Bilateral_Investment_Treaties/
index.asp (listing U.S. BITs in force) (last visited May 14, 2009).

74. Memorandum from Luke Eric Peterson and Mark Kantor, Vale
Columbia Center on Sustainable International Investment (Jan. 13, 2009)
(on file with author).

75. See id. for a list of cases, including CME v. Czech Republic (UNCI-
TRAL rules arbitration); Ronald Lauder v. Czech Republic (UNCITRAL
rules arbitration); European Media Ventures v. Czech Republic (pending
UNCITRAL rules arbitration); Victor Pey Casado and President Allende
Foundation v. Republic of Chile, ICSID case no. ARB/98/2 (W. Bank
2008).

76. Joseph C. Lemire v. Ukraine, ICSID case no. ARB/06/18 (W. Bank
pending).

77. Tokios Tokeles v. Ukraine, ICSID case no. ARB/02/18 (Wash. D.C), at
¶ 123.

78. U.S. Department of State, NAFTA Investor-State Arbitrations, available at http://www.state.gov/s/l/c3439.htm (last visited May 14, 2009).

79. See comments of the USTR that censorship typically "falls under the
purview of the State Department." Associated Press, Google Seeks Help,
June 26, 2007, available at http://www.theglobeandmail.com/servlet/story/
RTGAM.20070622.wgtcensor0622/BNStory/Technology ("Google sees
the dramatic increase in government Net censorship, particularly in Asia
and the Middle East, as a potential threat to its advertising-driven business
model, and wants government officials to consider the issue in economic,
rather than just political, terms").

80. Peter Scheer, California First Amendment Coalition, Acting Globally
and Locally: From Internet Censorship in China to a TRO against
Atherton, CA (2008), available at http://www.cfac.org/content/index.php/
cfac-news/report. The petition drew its arguments from a paper written by
Columbia law professor Tim Wu. See Wu, World Trade Law.

81. California First Amendment Coalition, Briefing Paper: China's Internet
Measures Violate Its WTO Obligations (2007), available at http://www.
cfac.org/content/litigation/CFACBriefing.pdf.

82. James Politi and Richard Waters, Google and Yahoo Tread Carefully in China Internet Row, Fin. Times, Aug. 22, 2008 (quoting a trade scholar as suggesting that "the administration may be reluctant to use the WTO to address what could be viewed as 'nontrade foreign policy objectives'").

83. Wu, World Trade Law.

84. See Eric Bangeman, EU May Begin Treating 'Net Censorship as a Trade Barrier, Ars Technica, Feb. 27, 2008, available at http://arstechnica. com/news.ars/post/20080227-eu-may-begin-treating-net-censorship-as-a-trade-barrier.html ("If adopted, [the] proposal would require the EU to classify any Internet censorship as a barrier to trade, and would require that the issue be raised in any trade negotiations.... The measure will now go to the European Council for consideration. The Council can either adopt the proposal as passed by Parliament or send it back with further amendments").

85. See Lee Becker et al., Enrollments Increase, with Slightly Higher Percentages of Male Students, Journalism & Mass Comm. J., Autumn 2008, at 198, 202 (noting that 2007 enrollment in graduate journalism and mass communication programs was 3,940). According to the Bureau of Labor Statistics, in 2007 there were 6,550 broadcast news analysts, 51,620 reporters and correspondents, and 105,920 editors, for a total of 164,090. U.S. Dep't of Labor, Occupational Employment and Wages, 2007, at Table 1, available at http://www.bls.gov/news.release/pdf/ocwage.pdf.

86. See Press Release, Inst. of Int'l Educ., Enrollment of Foreign Students in the U.S. Climbs in 2005–2006 (Nov. 13, 2006) (noting that 564,766 international students were enrolled in U.S. higher education institutions in the 2005–2006 school year).

87. Data provided by the Institute of International Education.

88. See Masao Miyoshi and Harry Harootunian, Learning Places: The Afterlives of Area Studies 2 (2002) ("Historically, area studies programs...originated in the immediate post–World War II era and sought to meet the necessity of gathering and providing information about the enemy")

89. Thomas Erdbrink, Iranian Authorities Detain U.S. Journalist, Wash. Post, Mar. 3, 2009, at A9.

90. Jill Drew and Maureen Fan, China Falls Short on Vows for Olympics, Wash. Post, Apr. 21, 2008, at A1.

91. China Eases Rules for Foreign Media, N.Y. Times, Oct. 18, 2008, at A7.

92. See Human Rights Council, Universal Periodic Review: Mexico (Feb. 10, 2009), available at http://www.ohchr.org/EN/HRBodies/UPR/Pages/Highlights10February2009am.aspx; Committee to Protect Journalists, Crime Photographer Shot Dead, Reporter Injured in Mexico (Feb. 17, 2009), available at http://cpj.org/2009/02/crime-photographer-shot-dead-reporter-injured-in-m.php.

93. Dean Graber, Mexico: Proposal Would Make Attacks on Journalists a Federal Crime, Knight Center for Journalism in the Americas: A News Blog (Nov. 27, 2008), available at http://knightcenter.utexas.edu/blog/?q=en/node/2365.

Index